Discover the Rocky Mountain Front

A Hiking Guide

By Tom Kotynski

RIVERBEND
PUBLISHING

GreatFalls**Tribune**
MEDIA

Dedication

To those who have worked untiringly for a wild Front: Gene Sentz, Bill Cunningham, Roy Jacobs, Stoney Burk, Dusty Crary, Karl Rappold, Tony Porcarelli, Chuck Blixrud, Joe Perry, Casey Perkins, Peter Aengst, Gabe Furshong, Holly Baker Wulf, Gerry Jennings, Mark Good, U.S. Senator Jon Tester, and former U.S. Senator Max Baucus.

Discover the Rocky Mountain Front: A Hiking Guide

Copyright © 2015 by the *Great Falls Tribune*

Published by Riverbend Publishing, Helena, Montana

ISBN: 978-1-60639-085-6

Printed in the USA

2 3 4 5 6 7 8 9 0 MG 22 21 20 19 18 17 16 15

Updated and revised Second Edition. The First Edition was published in 2006.

Text design by Sarah Cauble, www.sarahcauble.com
Maps created by Nick Daniels and Scott Sanford
Photos by Tom Kotynski

Front cover photo: Hikes on the Front offer spectacular views. This scene is from Rierdon Gulch Hike No. 15.

Back cover photo: Sawtooth climb, a sidetrip from the Home Gulch/Sun Canyon Hike No. 11.

Riverbend Publishing
P.O. Box 5833
Helena, MT 59604
1-866-787-2363
www.riverbendpublishing.com

Contents

The falls in spring along the Headquarters Pass trail.

Introduction

Much has happened since the First Edition of this book was published in 2006.

First, the great forest fires of 2007 carved up much of the area.

Then, a movement to protect the Front with wilderness designation coalesced, led by local residents and pushed by such organizations as the Coalition to Protect the Rocky Mountain Front and Montana Wilderness Association. They conceived a citizen's Rocky Mountain Front Heritage Act to protect the wild heritage of the Front.

They succeeded in persuading Congress and President Obama that an additional 67,112 acres in the Front should be added to the Bob Marshall Wilderness Area and another 208,160 acres be placed in a new category called, "Conservation Management Areas," that locks in the current uses that have made the Front the wild place that it is.

This covers an area from Falls Creek and the Dearborn River near Augusta north to Walling Reef near Dupuyer.

I was disappointed that more land wasn't designated wilderness. For starters, I'd love to see the Badger-Two Medicine be added. But, I was delighted to see that five particularly sensitive and deserving areas were recognized.

Who could argue that Our Lake and the areas leading up to Route and Headquarters Pass weren't wild enough to qualify? Or that Patrick's Basin, Falls Creek/Silver King or the West Fork Teton and Deep Creek additions didn't deserve such protection?

This book revisits, updates and adds to the hikes from the First Edition.

It will also look at those five areas added to the Bob Marshall and suggest hikes in each of the areas.

The Heritage Act is very much a work in progress. While it set aside those five areas and the total acreage amounts, it left to the Forest Service the task of setting wilderness boundaries taken from roughly drawn maps.

The "boundaries" I use here are those proposed by the act's authors and done in consultation with the Forest Service. They could very well change.

When the boundaries are set I will publish those changes online for users of this book. Look for updates on my Weblog: outtherewithtom.blogspot.com

Two things are certain, however, public access to the Bob Marshall Wilderness will now be much closer, and the Heritage Act is notable because it provides the authorization to attack the spread of noxious weeds along the Front.

This book also corrects some errors in the First Edition, most notably the directions to Muddy Creek Falls.

This new edition also corrects some hike distances, a task made much more easily with the emergence of GPS devices and digital topographical software.

Now it is up to you to get out and discover the Rocky Mountain Front!

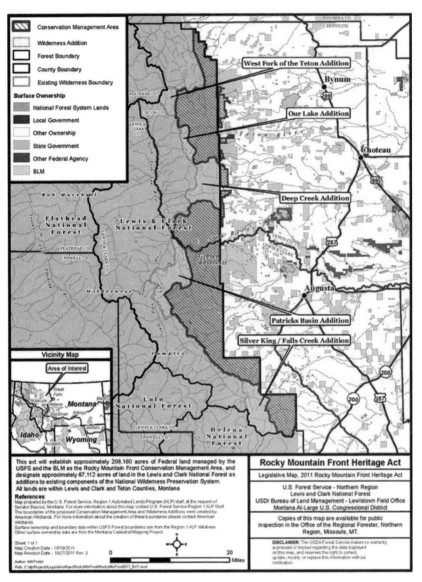

An preliminary version of Wilderness additions of the Rocky Mountain Front Heritage Act.

In the Patrick's Basin Addition to the Bob Marshall Wilderness.

Hiking New Wilderness

Access to the Bob Marshall and Scapegoat wilderness areas has gotten a whole lot easier with passage of the Rocky Mountain Front Heritage Act.

The act added five roadless areas totaling 67,112 acres in the Front to the Bob Marshall and Scapegoat, moving the boundaries of the wilderness closer to hikers, backpackers, snowshoers and backcountry skiers.

Dave Cunningham, information officer for the Lewis and Clark National Forest, pointed out that people have had easy access to these areas all along, but that they just weren't called, "wilderness."

It may be some time before the U.S. Forest Service finishes its review of boundaries and puts out a detailed map.

Rocky Mountain District Ranger Mike Munoz said that acreages in each of the areas, and which wilderness area, (the Bob or the Scapegoat) will have to be sorted out and approved by U.S. Secretary of Agriculture.

With what I can gather from looking at current maps and comparing them to the proposed boundaries in maps published by the Save the Front organization, here are descriptions of the five areas with some ideas on how to reach them, referencing hikes in this book.

Silver King/ Falls Creek

Think Dearborn River and the 6-mile round trip Devil's Glen hike (Trail No.

206) and you've reached the wilderness boundary, in this case the Scapegoat Wilderness, part of the Bob Marshall Complex. Walk the Continental Divide Trail between the Alice Creek headwaters and Caribou Peak and you will also be in the Scapegoat. (Hike No. 3)

Patrick's Basin

If you've ever climbed Patrol Mountain, the area immediately north and east nearly to the Benchmark Road, is now in the wilderness. You can now reach the wilderness boundary from the Benchmark Campground almost immediately when hiking the Straight Creek/Patrol Mountain Trail Nos. 212/213. Patrick Basin also contains other large mountains like Allen and Sheep Shed that would be part of the Bob Marshall. A major access is Lange Creek Trail No. 243. (reached via Trails 202,242 or from Gibson Reservoir). Under the bill, you'll be in the Bob and the Patrick Basin Addition nearly as soon as you cross the South Fork Sun Pack Bridge at Benchmark, Trail No. 202. (Hike No. 7)

Deep Creek

This addition is a land of great gulches and high peaks. The rule of thumb here is that if the creeks flow toward Deep Creek, it's in the Bob Marshall Wilderness. That would mean that hiking the Green Gulch/Reardon Gulch 14.25-mile loop (Trails No. 126,127,135) you'd be in the Bob along Slim and Sheep

Along the Continental Divide between Alice Creek and Caribou Mountain now puts you in the Silver King/Falls Creek Addition to the Scapegoat Wilderness.

gulches, but not Green and Readon gulches. Another way to reach this would be via Blacktail/Mortimer gulches from the Sun River Canyon area (Trails No. 223). (Hikes Nos. 13, 15)

Our Lake

This is probably the Front's most popular hike (Trail No. 184), but the wilderness boundary is moved closer to the parking area near the South Fork Teton, and includes the east side of Rocky Mountain peak, the highest mountain in the Bob. This addition also pushes the boundary closer to the trailheads of Headquarters Pass (Trail No. 165), and Route Creek Pass (Trail No. 108). (Hikes Nos. 16, 17)

In the West Fork Teton Addition to the Bob Marshall Wilderness above Washboard Reef.

West Fork Teton

Teton Just behind Mount Wright along Trail No. 114 to include the forks of the West Fork, like Wright and Olney creeks. The Wright Creek drainage, without a formal trail is particularly scenic with towering Mount Wright on the east and an extension of the limestone Corrugate Ridge to the west. Previously, the wilderness boundary had been at Teton Pass, a hike of 5.5-miles one way. That is a hike I'd highly recommend. (Hike No. 24)

The Heritage Act also designates 208,160 acres of the Front as "Conservation Management Areas," where the restrictive Forest Service Travel plans are now set into law. That means that much of the Front remains "de facto" wilderness without the title.

However, it would limit road-building while it protects current motorized recreation and public access for hunting, biking, timber-thinning and grazing.

And, importantly, the act prioritizes eradication and prevention of noxious weeds on the designated public lands. This, in turn, helps protect adjacent private lands.

Earlier, through the efforts of former U.S. Sens. Max Baucus and Conrad Burns and former Lewis and Clark National Forest supervisor Gloria Flora, the Front was withdrawn from oil and gas development.

The Heritage Act was passed through an amendment attached to the 2014 Defense Bill and represents a compromise supported by then U.S. Rep. Steve Daines, a Republican, and U.S. Sens. Jon Tester and John Walsh, both Democrats. It was signed into law by President Barack Obama.

Why choose the Rocky Mountain Front for your day hikes?

That's an often asked question by those familiar only with Glacier National Park or the Bob Marshall Wilderness complex.

They drive right by the Front on the way to the park or hurriedly cross it on their way into the Bob.

Those who ask that question may be intimidated by the Front's size, unfamiliar with access or just haven't taken the time to explore this 110-mile long, narrow band of mountains that gives hikers and climbers the vantage point to view the unusual zone where the mountains meet the Great Plains.

The choice of the Front has been an easy one for me. It is here where I can get away from the crowds in Glacier and the horse-intensive Bob Marshall.

The Front's precipitous peaks are the highest in the Bob Marshall complex and because of the sparse vegetation allow for tremendous, unblocked vistas.

On the eastern edge of the Rocky Mountains, the Front is affected by the rain shadow that provides boundless sun. The constant wind provides the ventilation necessary for pristine air.

It is here on the Front that the last Great Plains grizzlies roam. There are mountain goat, Bighorn sheep and vast herds of elk. The meadows and hillsides abound with wildflowers that blossom from April until the fall snows blanket them.

The mountains are such that nearly all peaks are reachable by easy climbs or scrambles making them accessible to the non-technical climber. But there are sheer walls that would challenge the elite rock-climber as well, which are being discovered by those who have begun putting up routes.

Up nearly every drainage there's a waterfall or two that gushes or plunges from its precipice.

I find myself asking the questioner, "Why not the Rocky Mountain Front?"

These mountains are in easy reach of the major Montana population centers of Great Falls and Helena, and increasingly I see license plates from Missoula, Kalispell and Bozeman at trailheads.

I'm hoping this hiking guide will encourage those intimidated by the Front's size to explore and enjoy.

I did many of these hikes with my children when they were young. They have also accompanied me on a number of the mountain climbs as well. As a senior citizen, I re-hike many of the trails and re-climb many of the peaks.

Another reason is that I'm very concerned about the wild future of the Rocky Mountain Front.

My hope is that this guide will help people discover this area and build a constituency that will fight for its wild preservation.

So, why not pick one of these hikes and find out why you should have tried the Front sooner?

Boundaries of the Front

Generally, many locals consider "The Front" to be the east-facing mountain slopes in the national forests where the Rockies meet the Great Plains between Marias Pass south of Glacier National Park and Rogers Pass near Lincoln.

But surely the Front must include those eastern slopes of Glacier from Divide to Chief Mountain peaks.

Sometimes when I drive west of Lincoln, I like to think the southern boundaries of the Scapegoat and Bob Marshall wilderness areas are part of the Front. Shouldn't those mountains in the Bob Marshall west of and adjacent to Swift Reservoir outside Dupuyer be considered part of the Front even though they are tucked inside the wilderness boundaries? What about the adjacent and intermingled private lands and other public lands such as those managed by the U.S. Bureau of Land Management and the state Department of Fish, Wildlife and Parks?

"We don't have a set definition for the Front," said Bonnie Dearing, former public information officer for the Lewis and Clark National Forest in Great Falls. "When we talk about it here, it is in general reference to our forest's Rocky Mountain Ranger District (Division) or parts of its management areas."

She rightly points out that "The Front" really stretches across public lands from Canada down through New Mexico. "It is the east side of the Front Range all the way up and down," she said.

Longtime wilderness advocate Bill Cunningham's boundaries are more poetic.

"The Front (as I loosely define here) stretches from Marias Pass 110 miles south to Rogers Pass and extends from the Continental Divide east to the 'Front of the Front' foothills interface with the Northern Great Plains. The source is somewhat arbitrary and is more a function of an 'east of the mountains' feeling (wind, eastward-leaning trees, limestone reefs, great canyon mouths, bound by sheer rock walls, along with a full complement of wild critters)," Cunningham, who now resides in Choteau, said.

Choteau schoolteacher, hiker and outfitter Gene Sentz has been crusading for the preservation of the Front for more than 35 years.

His definition has historical and ecological underpinnings.

"Defining the Front sounds easy, but it all depends on whom you ask, I guess," said Sentz. "I came to live in Choteau in 1970, and the first time I ever heard the mountains west of here called 'Rocky Mountain Front' was when the Lewis and Clark National Forest was doing a management plan in 1977. That term, 'Rocky Mountain Front,' was written on a draft environmental impact statement at that time, so I assume the Forest Service coined it, although maybe someone had used the term before — I'm not sure about that."

For the 1977 management plan, "Rocky Mountain Front" referred specifically to the national forest land in the Lewis and Clark National Forest east of the Bob Marshall and Scapegoat Wilderness boundary between Highway 2 on the north and the head of Falls Creek on the south, where the Lewis and Clark National Forest borders the Helena National Forest at the head of Alice Creek, he said.

"Now, it seems the Lewis and Clark National Forest prefers to call all its lands administered by the Choteau District ' the Rocky Mountain Division,' but that includes the national forest lands inside the wilderness too, so 'Rocky Mountain Front' is still what our 'Friends' network uses to define non-wilderness lands," said Sentz.

"I guess somewhere along the line, the term has been expanded to generally include all public lands outside of designated wilderness between Highway 2 and Highway 200 — so that would make 'Rocky Mountain Front' include Lewis and Clark National Forest lands, Helena National Forest lands in Alice Creek, all the U.S. Bureau of Land Management Outstanding Natural Areas along the Front bordering on national forest land and the state Wildlife Management Areas (WMA) too (i.e. Sun River WMA, Blackleaf WMA, Ear Mountain WMA)" he said.

Sentz pointed out that some people, especially state Fish, Wildlife and Parks biologists, might say that as wildlife winter range and habitat, a lot of the private land "along the Rocky Mountain Front" is as important as, or more important than, the public land. Of course, there are the Nature Conservancy's lands and Boone & Crockett ranch lands, plus an increasing amount of private land under conservation easements.

Mt. Frazier in the Front.

The Montana Wilderness Association, which has labored many years on protecting the Front for inclusion in the National Wilderness System, has thought this through and has a pretty good definition and boundaries, which makes you think about it in chunks, somewhat in the way alluded to by the Lewis and Clark's Dearing.

"When working on this issue, we describe 'The Front' as the roadless areas along the Front," said Brad Borst, former Rocky Mountain Front campaign coordinator for the MWA in Helena. Those areas have been identified over the years by various federal agencies as potential candidates for wilderness designation.

To steal a phrase from the U.S. Supreme Court on one landmark ruling, I might not be able to define 'The Front' but I know it when I see it.

Wind Mountain is a prime example of the Front's uplifted and folded geology.

Sections of the Front from north to south:

Badger-Two Medicine
U.S. Forest Service, approximately 125,700 acres

Choteau Mountain
USFS, approximately 26,500 acres

Choteau Mountain Face
U.S. Bureau of Land Management, approximately 5,000 acres

Teton Peaks
USFS, approximately 26,100 acres

Deep Creek
USFS, approximately 59,600 acres

Deep Creek Face
BLM, approximately 7,200 acres

Sawtooth Ridge
USFS, approximately 14,900 acres

Renshaw Mountain
USFS, approximately 54,500 acres

Crown Mountain
USFS, approximately 33,200 acres

Falls Creek
USFS, approximately 36,200 acres

Silver King
USFS, approximately 26,800 acres

Access to the Front

There was a time when I was intimidated by the Rocky Mountain Front. When I first moved to Great Falls, the Front seemed impenetrable, so forbidding that I preferred to bypass it in favor of going to the more "civilized" Glacier National Park with its paved roads.

The crudely marked, rocky and dusty roads which lead to the mysterious mountains on the horizon west of Great Falls confused me. Their length discouraged me. My map-reading skills and the Forest Service's maps made my early trips to the Front a matter of happenstance.

The vastness of the Front, which stretches from East Glacier Park down to Lincoln, was overwhelming. I would look at the map and become bewildered not only by the problems of access, but choice.

So what follows is an outline on how to get to the Rocky Mountain Front for whatever you plan to do: a Sunday drive, camping, a picnic, a hike or a fishing trip. There are also some suggestions on hikes.

Main Access Points

The main access points are through Augusta or Choteau, both less than an hour's drive from Great Falls.

Both are reached by taking I-15 to the Vaughn exit, traveling west on Montana 200. At the junction, a mile before Sun River, take U.S. 89 north to Choteau. If you're going to Augusta, continue on 200 through Sun River to Simms. At Simms leave 200 and continue west on Highway 21 to Augusta.

What is Wilderness?

The Wilderness Act, signed into law in 1964, created the National Wilderness Preservation System and recognized wilderness as "an area where the earth and its community of life are untrammeled by man, where man himself is a visitor who does not remain." The Act further defined wilderness as "an area of undeveloped Federal land retaining its primeval character and influence without permanent improvements or human habitation, which is protected and managed so as to preserve its natural conditions . . . ."

Congress has now designated more than 106 million acres of federal public lands as wilderness: 44 million of these acres are in 47 parks and total 53 percent of National Park System lands. Additional national park areas are managed as "recommended" or "proposed" wilderness until Congress acts on their status.

Rogers Pass trailhead is easy to find.

There is worthwhile access along Forest Service roads out of Bynum (Blackleaf Canyon-Muddy Creek Falls) and Dupuyer (Swift Reservoir-Birch Creek, North Fork Dupuyer Creek) and Heart Butte (Palookaville and Badger Creek) as well. On the north, Highway 2 delivers you to Marias Pass; on the south, Montana 200 to Rogers Pass.

What you'll need is a picnic lunch you can carry in a day pack, comfortable shoes (canvas tennis or running shoes will do), some trail snacks, a canteen, water bottle or hydration pack for drinking water, rain gear and a light coat for changeable weather.

It is best to be on the trail by 10 a.m., so you can be out before dark with the children.

I suggest stopping at the Lewis and Clark National Forest ranger stations in Choteau or Augusta or the forest headquarters in Great Falls at 1101 15th St. N. for maps and information. Don't hesitate to pull over and ask someone should you get confused.

From south to north, here are the access points and what you'll see when you get there:

Rogers Pass

Highway 200, 66 miles west of Great Falls. Good two-lane highway with views of the Front all the way. The pass is at 5,610 feet where you'll find access to the Continental Divide Trail on both sides of the road. To the south is Rogers Peak, Anaconda Hill and eventually Flesher Pass; to the north, it is 40 minutes to the ridgeline that wanders to Cadotte Pass, Green and Red Mountains and eventually Lewis and Clark Pass. Views of the Great Plains and Front to the east; heavy forest and headwaters of the Blackfoot River to the west.

Augusta Area

Dearborn River/Falls Creek

Pick up Highway 434 in Augusta and take it 14 miles south to Bean Lake turnoff. Take the turn and it is another 6 miles to the Dearborn River Trailhead No. 206 parking area and trailhead. This trail delivers you to the Dearborn's most scenic fishing holes and ultimately into the Scapegoat Wilderness. Falls Creek Trailhead No. 229 is about 4 miles beyond the Bean Lake turnoff (and just beyond the former Diamond Bar X resort). However, this trail is curently closed due to access issues accross private land.

Elk Creek

Continue south through Augusta on Highway 434. The Elk Creek Road comes in at 6 miles from the west. This is the road to the Steamboat (former) lookout Trail No. 205 and Cataract Falls. The road is 12 miles from the junction of Highway 434. Cataract Falls is a couple of hundred feet from the parking area at the end of the road.

Smith Creek

Pick up Highway 434 in Augusta. The Smith Creek Road is 4 miles southwest of town. Proceed about 11 miles, going past Haystack Butte, to the Smith Creek Trailhead No. 215 that begins on a heavily grazed, logged and burned ranch. It is about 2 miles to Smith Creek Falls and eventually to the Welcome Pass and Crown Mountain trailheads, major jumping-off points into the Scapegoat Wilderness

How is wilderness different from other federal public lands?

Designated wilderness is the highest level of conservation protection for federal lands. Only Congress may designate wilderness or change the status of wilderness areas. Wilderness areas are designated within existing federal public land. Congress has directed four federal land management agencies—U.S. Forest Service, Bureau of Land Management, U.S. Fish and Wildlife Service, and National Park Service—to manage wilderness areas so as to preserve and, where possible, to restore their wilderness character.

The Wilderness Act prohibits permanent roads and commercial enterprises, except commercial services that may provide for recreational or other purposes of the Wilderness Act. Wilderness areas generally do not allow motorized equipment, motor vehicles, mechanical transport, temporary roads, permanent structures or installations (with exceptions in Alaska). Wilderness areas are to be primarily affected by the forces of nature.

Benchmark

In Augusta, look for a sign directing you to the Benchmark Road. It is 32 miles of gravel all the way to its end at the South Fork of the Sun River trailhead, a major access point into the Bob Marshall Wilderness. Some sights to look for along the way:

Nilan Reservoir, Crown and Patrol mountains trailheads, Wood Lake, Benchmark campground, Fairview and Renshaw Lake trailheads. At mile 13 look for the turnoff to the Willow-Beaver Creek Road, which eventually will take you to Gibson Dam in the Sun Canyon.

Sun River Canyon/Gibson Dam

In Augusta, look for the Sun Canyon Road access sign. The 26-mile road winds across the plains, past Willow Creek Reservoir, the Sun River Game Range (home to more than 1,000 elk in winter), and into a canyon flanked by Sawtooth and Castle Reef mountains on either side of the road. This is the major access to Gibson Reservoir as well as the Sun Canyon Lodge and several dude ranches where it is possible to rent horses, spend some cabin time or outfit your wilderness trip. Campgrounds include Home Gulch and Mortimer Gulch sites. There is a scenic overlook above Gibson Dam. There are trailheads around the north side of Gibson reservoir into the Sun River country of the Bob Marshall and up many of the parallel gulches like Big George, Mortimer, Blacktail, Hannan, Home, and Norwegian. A charming day hike is a short

Bighorn sheep in Wagner Basin in the Sun River Canyon.

walk into Wagner Basin accessed from Hannan Gulch. It's .3 miles to the road (turn right) that takes you to a parking area beyond a cluster of cabins (another .4 miles). It is about a 10-minute walk from a faint trailhead into the basin, where you'll find spectacular scenery and a large herd of bighorn sheep.

Willow/Beaver Creek Road

A scenic 12-mile connecting road between the Sun River Canyon and Benchmark Road. The road is closed during hunting season and winter. It is also the access point to the popular Willow Creek Falls area and a great way to gain access to Fairview Mountain. You pass the Girl Scouts' Camp Scoutana on this road, too.

Choteau Area

Teton Canyon/County Road

Find this road 6 miles north of Choteau off U.S. 89. It is two-lane paved to the national forest boundary, about 20 miles, and then good gravel to its end at the West Fork of the Teton, another 10 miles away. The road provides spectacular views of the Front all the way, particularly Ear and Choteau mountains. It provides access to the Teton Pass Ski Area, Middle Fork of the Teton Trailhead and 7 Lazy P dude ranch, Jones Creek, Clary Coulee, North Fork, Waldron Creek, West Fork trailheads and the South Fork Road (see next page).

South Fork Road

The South Fork Road comes in from the south on the Teton Road at about mile 16. It becomes gravel, crosses the Teton River and winds its way through the South Fork canyon for nearly 10 miles to its end at the Our Lake/Headquarters Pass trailhead. Along the way you'll pass the BLM's Ear Mountain trailhead and trailheads for Green and Rierdon gulches, South Fork trail and the Lonesome Ridge trail cutoff to the Middle Fork of the Teton.

Bynum

Blackleaf Canyon/Muddy Creek

Take U.S. 89 to the town of Bynum. Turn left when you see the old one-room schoolhouse. You're on the Blackleaf Canyon Road, a good gravel road that travels some 15 miles back to the Trail No. 106.

To reach Muddy Creek Falls from Bynum, do the following:

What is the significance of wilderness?

Through the Wilderness Act, Congress recognized the intrinsic value of wild lands. Some of the tangible and intangible values mentioned in the Wilderness Act include "solitude or a primitive and unconfined type of recreation," as well as "ecological, geological, or other features of scientific, educational, scenic, or historical value." Wilderness areas provide habitat for wildlife and plants, including endangered and threatened species.

Wilderness protects open space, watersheds, natural soundscapes, diverse ecosystems and biodiversity. The literature of wilderness experience frequently cites the inspirational and spiritual values of wilderness, including opportunities to reflect on the community of life and the human place on Earth. Wilderness provides a sense of wildness, which can be valuable to people whether or not those individuals actually visit wilderness. Just knowing that wilderness exists can produce a sense of curiosity, inspiration, renewal and hope.

(Excerpted from U.S. Park Service website: wilderness.nps.gov/faqnew.cfm)

Sun Canyon Lodge offers dude rides above Home Gulch.
That's Castle Reef in the background.

Out of Bynum travel up the Blackleaf Road 13.9 miles to the Blackleaf Wildlife Management Area road juncture. Turn left (west) and drive 1 mile to the Blackleaf sign. Turn left (south) and proceed 1.4 miles. Turn right and go .5 miles and turn right onto a two track road. Another .2 miles and you'll reach an arched gate. Travel 2 miles on this road to an obvious parking area where there's a locked gate. Get out and walk 2 miles to the falls along the creek bottom.

Dupuyer

Swift Reservoir

Look for the state Department of Transportation rest stop north of Dupuyer on U.S. 89. The good gravel Forest Service access road goes 18 miles back to a BLM campground and parking area for trails around the south side of Swift Reservoir. It is possible to go around the north side as well, but the road is rough and rutted. Walling Reef south of the reservoir, and Mount Richmond, directly above the reservoir, dominate the skyline. All trails on both sides of the reservoir lead into the Bob Marshall Wilderness along the South, Middle and North forks of Birch Creek.

North Fork Dupuyer Canyon/ Boone And Crockett Ranch Country

To reach the trailhead you take the road west out of Dupuyer that runs by the new post office, passing through the Boone and Crockett Teddy Roosevelt Ranch. The road continues south and east of the headquarters and then heads west toward the canyon. The last 7 miles of road are quite sketchy. There are 4 gates and 4 creek crossings and some pretty deep ruts and mud holes. This is not the kind of country you want to take the family car.

Heart Butte
Palookaville

From the Blackfeet Reservation town of Heart Butte take the Heart Butte-Browning Road north about 8 miles to Little Badger Creek. Just north of the creek there's a road with a paved turnout coming in from the west. Take that about a 1.5 miles where you'll see a ranch house. There's a dirt track road there with the brown Forest Service road sign No. 9128 on it. Follow that about 4.5 miles where it intersects with a short road that drops to the trailhead. You'll find Forest Service Trail No. 172. The road you just left continues to the top of Mount Baldy! It is used to service the electronics equipment on the mountaintop and is sporadically closed. Trail No. 172 is located in a place called "Palookaville" and is the jumping off point for Kiyo Crag Lake. There is limited access to Badger Creek Canyon.

Walking the Mount Lockhart ridge line.

East Glacier Park
Marias Pass

About 9 miles west of East Glacier Park on U.S. 2. The lowest point across the Continental Divide at 5,280 feet. Provides access to Flattop and Elk Calf mountains and the South Fork of the Two Medicine River trailheads. About 150 miles northwest of Great Falls.

Should concerns about grizzlies keep you away from the Front?

I don't think so. I've been hiking and climbing off trail there for more than 40 years and have seen grizzlies only three times and at a good distance. I've seen their signs, so I know they are there, but they are shy and try to avoid humans. They are not like the bears in Yellowstone and Glacier that deal with vast crowds. The key is to follow good grizzly bear country country etiquette.

⚠ Here are some tips:

- Carry bear spray and know how to use it. This means firing test shots.

- Make plenty of noise.

- Travel in groups.

- Don't get between a female grizzly and her cubs.

- If you encounter a grizzly, don't panic, but slowly back away. If attacked, drop to a fetal position with your hands behind your neck and protect your vital organs.

- Know the difference between a black and a grizzly bear.

A black bear can have light brown fur like a grizzly; only the grizzly has the disk-like face, the long claws and the pronounced hump on its back. A grizzly is more aggressive, while a black bear, unless with cubs, usually flees human encounters.

- Camp cleanly. Cook away from your sleeping area. Suspend your pack and food from a tree at least 12 feet in the air, away from and above the grasp of animals.

- Don't bring food of any kind into your tent.

It's always wise to be cautious and alert in grizzly country, but knowing the bears are there shouldn't keep you from venturing out. So, go into the Front and experience its wildness, a wildness enhanced by the knowledge that the great bear is there.

Grizzlies roam the Rocky Mountain Front.

Mount Frazier from the Blackleaf Canyon Trail.

How to Use this Book

The goal of this book is to help people get into and enjoy the Rocky Mountain Front.

I had long heard that the Front was inaccessible because of poor access and lack of amenities.

As you read this book, you'll come to find that access is good and plentiful, and there are numerous campgrounds, trailheads, outfitters and even some small businesses to serve a growing number of visitors.

This book is not an exhaustive compendium of every trail in the Front, but it contains every major access point, trailhead and all the major scenic attractions.

There are enough hikes and sights included here to keep most people busy and active for a lifetime.

To help you choose and enjoy the trails, I have used a 1 to 5 difficulty rating, with 1 being easiest and 5 being hardest. Length and elevation gain are the main criteria.

An **Easy** hike—hike—numbered 1 or 2—would be one that is less than 3 miles long, contains less than 800 feet of elevation gain and loss, and is easy to follow.

A **Moderate** hike—numbered 3—would be 3 to 7 miles long, usually gaining elevation in steady ascents with perhaps a few short, steep pitches.

A **More Difficult** hike—numbered 4—would be 5 to 12 miles long and gain significant elevation, often 2,000 to 3,500 feet, in long, steep sections.

A **Strenuous** hike—numbered 5— gains the most elevation, sometimes more than 4,000 feet, in long, steep, challenging ascents. Number 5 hikes often involve off-trail travel.

It is difficult to rate hikes because what might be easy for one person is moderate or strenuous for another. If you are just starting to hike, begin with the Easy hikes and work your way up through the Moderate and Strenuous hikes.

Remember that as you go into the forest or start up a mountain, you should be prepared for this strenuous activity and realize that changing weather, wild animals or potential hazards (such as washed-out trails) could have a bearing on what you will accomplish. There is no way to warn you about all hazards in the Rocky Mountain Front.

I always advise a cautious approach. If the weather changes drastically or you feel you are approaching your physical limit, back off. The trail will always be there and you can return.

Most folks can comfortably travel at a 2 mph pace on good trail. That can slow in steep terrain or if you are carrying a heavy pack. If climbing, factor in about an hour of climbing for every 1,000 feet of elevation gained.

There is no substitute for having a good map for the area you've selected to visit and knowing how to read it. This is particularly true if you have a hankering to climb one of the Front's spectacular mountains, which often requires going off trail.

However, I have found a GPS helpful, if expensive and with a high learning curve. But it can track where you're at in real time, recording distances traveled, elevations gained and lost.

Enjoying the Ear Mountain trail hike.

Hikes Rated by Difficulty

1 & 2 Easy

1. Rogers Pass 2
12. Wagner Basin 1
14. Ear Mountain to Yeager Flats 2
21. Jones Creek 2
25. Muddy Creek Falls 2
27. Blackleaf Canyon 1
28. North Fork Dupuyer Canyon 1

3 Moderate

2. Devil's Glen
9. Willow Creek Falls
11. Home Gulch
13. Mortimer Gulch
16. Headquarters Pass
17. Our Lake
20. Route Creek Pass/Middle Fork Teton
22. North Fork Teton River Canyon
29. Swift Dam
30. North Fork Birch Creek
31. Kiyo Crag Lake

4 More Difficult

3. Falls Creek from the Alice Creek Trailhead
4. Steamboat Mountain
5. Petty/Crown Creek Loop
7. Patrol Mountain
8. Renshaw Lake Loop
10. Lime Gulch
23. Mount Wright
24. Teton Pass
26. Blindhorse
32. Marias Pass

5 Strenuous

6. Crown Mountain
11. Home Gulch if Sawtooth Mountain is climbed
14. Ear Mountain if the mountain is climbed
15. Rierdon/Green Gulch Loop
18. Rocky Mountain Peak
19. Clary to Blackleaf

Hike Locations
The 32 hikes numbered from south to north

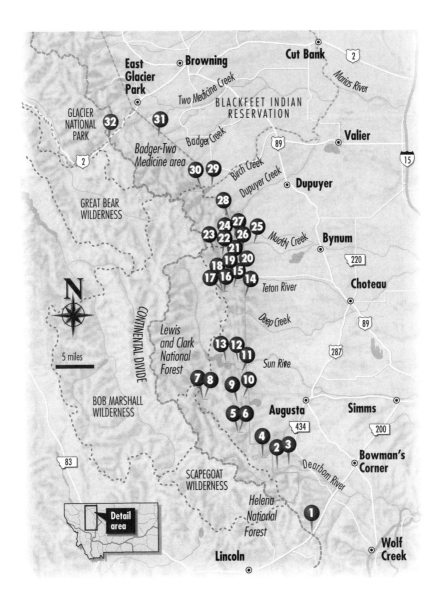

The author on top of Choteau Mountain. (Jim Heckel photo)

Continental Divide Trail near Rogers Pass.

If the Rocky Mountain Front is defined by boundaries that go from Rogers to Marias passes, a good place to begin experiencing it is at Rogers Pass (elevation 5,610 feet) on its south end.

This pass is reachable from Great Falls in about an hour on Highway 200. For many years I've always factored in the time to do this hike on my way west to Missoula or the West Coast.

It has a historical aspect to it: the coldest temperature in the lower 48 states at 80 below zero was recorded here on Jan. 20, 1954.

It is also an easy place to reach Continental Divide Trail No. 440 at the Rogers Pass sign. You'll know you're there if you see a short flight of wooden steps.

The trail switchbacks for 1.1 miles and gains about 800 feet to a small rock outcropping through timber and a brief opening of grass.

If you decide to go further, it is a nice open walk, but the terrain pitches and rolls as you approach various passes, like Cadotte, or mountains, like Red and Green.

It is possible to reach historic Lewis and Clark Pass from here where the Corps of Discovery crossed the mountains on the way back home and where Indian travois marks are still visible. It would be about an 8-mile hike with lots of elevation gain and loss. My recommendation is to leave a car at Alice Creek trailhead for Trail No. 440 if you decide to walk through.

As anywhere on the Front, wind can be a factor. Be prepared to be blown around.

Particularly during the winter I like to ski up from the pass on the other (east) side of the pass toward Rogers

Peak (elevation 7,043 feet). It travels through deep forest and climbs steeply through more forest until reaching the bare, grassy top and rock outcroppings. Here there are great views of the plains, Front and west-side mountain ranges.

However, the vistas and access are so superb that after you take this hike once, you'll wonder how you ever whizzed by without stopping your car for an interesting day hike no matter how many times you take it.

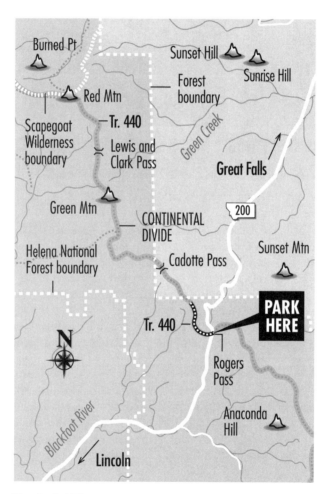

How to Get There

Rogers Pass is 66 miles west of Great Falls on Highway 200. The pass and trailhead are well marked. Look for a stairway on the right side of the road going toward Lincoln. It leads to Forest Service Trail No. 440, the Continental Divide Trail.

1 Rogers Pass

Distance
A little more than 2.2 miles from the pass to the high point and back.

 Difficulty
Easy. On a scale of 1-5, with 1 being easiest, about a 2 because the trail can be steep in spots, and 800 feet is gained.

Time Needed
About 45 minutes to an hour each way from the pass to the top.

Best Time
Any time the trail is clear of snow is good, but the most glorious time to hike to the top is in early June when the wildflowers are in bloom. There are vast fields of miniature blue, fragrant forget-me-nots at this time. I've also seen hundreds of bluebirds here when looking at the flowers. In early summer it is an easy spot to find beargrass.

 What You'll See
Fabulous views of the Front to the north, the Great Plains to the east and the heavily timbered headwaters of the Blackfoot River to the west. Elk and deer frequent this area.

Cautions
No drinking water. Changeable weather. Grizzly country.

 Sidetrips
Follow the Continental Divide Trail 8 miles west to Lewis and Clark Pass or cross the highway at Rogers Pass and climb 1,400 feet to Rodgers Peak.

Camping
Primitive in the national forest. Nearest campground is Aspen Grove Campground, 6 miles east of Lincoln on the Blackfoot River with 20 sites.

 Cross Country Skiing
Possible, particularly on Continental Divide Trail on east side of road.

 Maps
Helena National Forest, Rogers Pass, Stemple Pass, USGS topographic maps, Bob Marshall, Great Bear and Scapegoat Wilderness Complex Forest Service Map (small portion of Rogers pass included).

 Contacts
Helena National Forest Lincoln Ranger District: (406) 362-4265.

Bright red outcrops of rock along the Rogers Pass section of the Continental Divide Trail.

Fields of Forget-Me-Not alpine wildflowers bloom above Rogers Pass on the Continental Divide in mid-June.

Devil's Glen's translucent, clear turquoise waters rush through limestone canyons.

If the devil resides here, he's got it pretty cushy.

The Devil's Glen is where the Dearborn River drops and narrows and its emerald waters are forced through limestone chutes and multiple cascades.

It sits at the base of towering Steamboat Mountain (elevation 8,286 feet)—really a wall-like ridge that dominates the valley.

This is a main trail into the Scapegoat Wilderness Area, but only a fool would rush through it on the way there, ignoring its many fishing holes, waterfalls and backpack campsites.

Although the trail also serves the nearby C Bar N Wilderness Bible Camp, it never seems crowded despite the ease of access and its easy hiking terrain.

Trailhead No. 206 begins where the Dearborn River Road is gated, about 24 miles from Augusta.

Signs demand that hikers stay on the trail, which much of the way is only feet from that road, which gives access to private cabins.

Even across the Dearborn River bridge you are on private land until hitting the Lewis and Clark National Forest sign at a small, unnamed stream that crosses
the trail.

Once you cross the bridge, the high mountain country explodes. That's Steamboat Mountain to the north. On the south, Twin Buttes (elevation 7,532 and 7,231 feet).

Past that bridge the trail ascends a couple hundred feet, switchbacks and levels out above the stream.

Past the national forest sign it loses the elevation, taking the hiker within reach of the Dearborn, gushing and burbling below.

Once in sight, start looking for spots to play on the limestone, which serves as riverbank. There are numerous picnic and sunbathing spots to be had, but be careful near the cold, swift water. The stream is also known for its rainbow trout fishing holes.

This is really the beginning of some of the best backpacking campsites on the Front.

It is about 3.5 miles to Devil's Glen from where you parked.

In the winter after heavy, successive snows, this is a nice cross-country ski destination, too.

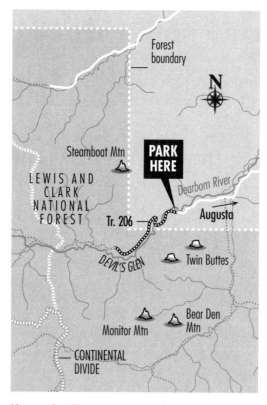

How to Get There

From Augusta, take State Highway No. 434 16 miles to the Bean Lake turnoff. Proceed about 8 miles to the end of the road where there's a gate across the road and the Trailhead No. 206 parking lot. The trail parallels the road for about a mile, where it crosses the Dearborn River bridge. You're still on private land here until you reach the Lewis and Clark National Forest sign, about another half-mile.

2 Devil's Glen

 Distance
7 miles roundtrip from the parking area.

 Difficulty
Moderate to easy with some elevation gain and loss as you climb up and back from the river.

 Time Needed
3-5 hours.

 Best Time
This hike is possible year-round, but is best from June through late October.

 What You'll See
Gorgeous views of translucent emerald Dearborn River that runs through limestone cliffs at the base of Steamboat Mountain and Twin Buttes on the south side. Small waterfalls drop off into deep pools. Great trout fishing.

This hike is within the new Falls Creek/Silver King addition to the Scapegoat Wilderness.

 Cautions
Weather, grizzly country, horse traffic.

 Sidetrips
An off-trail climb of Steamboat Mountain is possible at a point just beyond an unnamed stream that comes in at the forest boundary sign. A small pile of rocks marks a game-trail route. There are other of these small "ducks" on this path. This is a rugged 3,000+ foot approach.

 Camping
There are 6 campsites at Bean Lake on the Dearborn Road you'll use to approach this area.

 Maps
Lewis and Clark National Forest Visitors Map (1988), Bob Marshall, Great Bear, and Scapegoat Wilderness Complex Map (2011). Bean Lake and Steamboat USGS topographic maps.

 Contacts
Lewis and Clark National Forest Augusta Information Station (406) 562-3247, Choteau Ranger District (406) 466-5341, Supervisor's office in Great Falls, 791-7700.

Looking down the Dearborn River.

There are several falls that make up the Devil's Glen.

One of the many small waterfalls on Falls Creek.

Editor's Note: As of this writing, the access to this area from the Dearborn River Canyon has been closed by a private landowner. Do not attempt to access Trail No. 229 from the Dearborn Canyon. Access to Trail No. 219 and the Falls Creek area is available from the Alice Creek Trailhead near Lincoln, Montana. However, since the Forest Service continues to pursue access to Trail No. 229 from the Dearborn River Canyon, we have included information about Trail No. 229 in this edition, in anticipation of future access.

Falls Creek is the (undeservedly) neglected stepchild in the Dearborn River area.

It is overshadowed (quite literally) by the massive Steamboat Mountain that rises straight up from the Dearborn, which runs in green translucence through limestone canyons below.

It was also badly burned in 1988 by the Canyon Creek Fire, Montana's most massive blaze the year that Yellowstone went up in flames.

This area has also been a battleground between the wilderness and development forces which has resulted in a stalemate and de facto wilderness status. It is truly wild country.

The creek, named for its numerous cascades, is the area's heart, although mountains such as Table, Twin Buttes, Monitor, Blowout and Caribou peaks are certainly a draw. Local anglers attest to the creek's productivity.

You'll find yourself more interested in the Canyon Creek burn than repulsed by it. There is ample new growth, and the openings created by the fire provide better vistas of stark, spectacular mountains.

Trail No. 229 is the main artery through the area to the Continental Divide. Caribou Mountain at 8,755 feet is the largest mountain, towering some 4,000 feet above the valley floor where the Middle and West forks meet.

On one beautiful weekend my plan was to walk a traverse of about 10 miles around Table Mountain, elevation 7,163 feet, by taking Trail 229 to where the East Fork joins Falls Creek at Trail 219. The plan was to proceed up Table Mountain's southeast flank and around its east side, passing through Joslin and Cuniff basins and back to the Diamond Bar X Ranch.

Only I got tempted by Caribou Peak and continued up Falls Creek to its junction with its Middle Fork, where I left the trail and ascended the ridge off trail to the top of the mountain, with an eagle's-perch view of the entire Falls Creek area.

There was also the option of taking the Middle Fork to the Continental Divide through heavy timber and the mosaic of the burn, but I opted for that another day. With the current closure of access to the trail No. 229 trailhead, the upper Falls Creek area can be reached via the Continental Divide Trail by way of the Alice Creek trail accessed off Montana 200 outside Lincoln. This is

How To Get There:
Alternate Route

Alternate directions to reach the Falls Creek drainage from the south and over the Continental Divide: Out of Great Falls, take Highway 200 west toward Rogers Pass. The Alice Creek Road, which is pretty well marked by a Forest Service sign, is about 10 miles south of the pass on 200. Take a right (north) on the road. The Alice Creek trailhead is another 10 miles from the turn. There is a good parking and picnic area here. You're looking for Trail 493 here (looks like an old road). This heads toward Lewis and Clark Pass. At the pass, Trail 440, the Continental Divide Trail intersects. Take it toward Red Mountain and the divide above the East Fork of Falls Creek, where you can pick up Trail 219. If you enter the Falls Creek drainage this way, remember there is no easy access out to the Dearborn River.

LEWIS AND CLARK NATIONAL FOREST

Tr. 219

Red Mtn

Tr. 440

HELENA NATIONAL FOREST

Tr. 440
Continental
Divide Trail

Alice Creek Basin

Alice Creek Ranger Cabin

Tr. 493

Alice Creek

Lewis and Clark Pass

PARK HERE

CONTINENTAL DIVIDE

3 Falls Creek

 Distance

Alice Creek access: The hike from the Alice Creek trailhead to Red Mountain and to the junction of Trail 219 on the East Fork Falls Creek is 3.25 miles. This brings the hiker into the Falls Creek area at the headwaters of the East Fork of Falls Creek. Remember, if you walk in you won't be able at this writing to walk through to the Dearborn, but you will be able to access other Falls Creek trails. This would be a backpack rather than a hike.

Dearborn River access: This access using Trail #229 is currently closed. If access is re-opened, it is a mile to the trailhead from the gate. A logical spot to turn around on an exploratory hike would be where the East Fork meets the West Fork, about 3 miles from the gate. That would give you plenty to see.

 Difficulty

Alice Creek access: Strenuous, with an elevation gain of 1,655 feet.

Dearborn River access: Moderate, depending on the distance. The most difficult thing on this mostly flat trail is a couple of major crossings of Falls Creek, particularly during spring runoff.

 Time Needed

Alice Creek access: An overnight backpack.

Dearborn River access: 4-6 hours.

 Best Time

Spring through late fall, although it is possible to enjoy the area in the winter.

 What You'll See

A spectacularly secluded area that features scenery similar to that found along the Dearborn River, into which Falls Creek flows. As its name indicates, there are numerous small waterfalls in the creek. Rising in all directions are spectacular mountain peaks. This is one of the areas most heavily affected by the Canyon Creek Fire in 1988. The burn is quite evident. This area has also been a battleground between those who want it set aside for wilderness and those who think it has a potential for oil and gas development.

3 Falls Creek

 Cautions
Stream crossings, grizzly country, changeable weather, lack of good trail signage.

 Sidetrips
There are some very easy mountains in the area to climb off-trail including Twin Buttes, Table, Bear Den and Monitor. (See chapter on mountain climbing)

 Camping
Bean Lake has campsites nearby.

 Maps
Bob Marshall, Great Bear and Scapegoat Wilderness Complex map; USGS Topographic maps: Bean Lake, Blowout Mountain, Caribou Mountain.

 Contacts
Lewis and Clark National Forest station in Augusta, (406) 562-3247 or the supervisor's office in Great Falls, 791-7700. Helena National Forest Lincoln Ranger Station, 362-4265.

the preferred route during the access closure.

For hikers venturing onto Trail 229, keep in mind that you will cross and recross Falls Creek. Getting to Caribou Peak, I did so 6 times in each direction.

I would recommend an exploratory excursion into the area up Trail 229, stopping to enjoy the creek and the many falls that give it its appropriate name. Once you've done that, look at the map and figure out some fun day-hike or backpacking loops.

Unfortunately, some very selfish and destructive people have obliterated every trail sign along Trail 229, making it more difficult to figure out where to go up the East or Middle Forks or where the West Fork begins. Carry a good map and know how to read it.

4 Steamboat Mountain

The Steamboat ridge looking west to Steamboat lookout mountain.

This is really a climb, by good trail, to the top of what used to be the Steamboat Lookout. It sits on the northwest end of the several-miles-long Steamboat Mountain ridge. At 8,565 feet, it is higher than the named peak at the southeast end of the ridge at 8,286 feet. There's little left of the lookout other than some debris and a marker memorializing a Great Falls teen killed in a tragic accident.

The summit affords spectacular views of the Scapegoat Wilderness Area and the high peak, Scapegoat (elevation 9,202 feet), for which it is named.

This trail is also one of the best places in the Front to get the full extent of the Canyon Creek Fire of 1988 that raced through this spot in August of that year on the way to burning more than 240,000 acres.

As of this writing some 27 years later,

there's still plenty of scorched earth and burned trees to see. What's truly impressive is the new growth that abounds. There are patches of purple fireweed, which break up the green.

There is a tremendous amount of variety on this hike. The forest changes as you proceed up, progressively through aspen meadows, lodgepole and spruce stands.

From the parking lot you proceed through wildflower-covered meadows up to the base of Elk Creek Pass, where the trail forks. Stay high and to the left on Trail No. 205. There is a small pothole lake here that has been dry in recent years.

Then it's up through the trees beneath Steamboat's limestone cliffs.

Below the cliffs there's another trail junction. This time you'll take the trail to the left, No. 239, which you'll follow to the top of the old lookout.

Look around for fresh sign of elk on this trail. In year's past I've seen numbers of elk on the grassy hillsides below the cliffs, and a grizzly digging on the ridgeline.

You top out above timberline, switchbacking to a limestone ridge that takes you to the summit.

Plan to spend some time on top where you'll find satisfying and sweeping views of the Scapegoat Wilderness Area and Canyon Creek Fire.

It is possible (but taxing) to walk the ridgeline east several miles to the named Steamboat summit and make a point-to-point hike out of it by dropping down to the Dearborn River and out.

But get an early start. I've spent a long, cold night up on this mountain when I miscalculated that walk.

How to Get There

From Augusta, take Road 434 as if you are going to the Dearborn River. About 6 miles out of Augusta, start looking for the Elk Creek Road, 6 miles south of town. There's a good road sign. Turn west onto this good, unpaved road and drive 14 miles to its end, where you'll find Trail No. 205 and a good parking area.

4 Steamboat Mountain

 Distance
12 miles round trip.

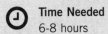 **Difficulty**
More difficult, a 4 on a scale of 5, with 5 being the hardest. Elevation gain is about 3,400 feet, and it is 6 miles each way, which makes this a significant day hike.

 Time Needed
6-8 hours

 Best Time
As soon as the snow and ice clears from the trail.

 What You'll See
Sweeping view of the Scapegoat Wilderness Area, the Canyon Creek Fire area, the Great Plains to the east.

 Cautions
Grizzly country.

Sidetrips
Cataract Falls within earshot and a couple hundred feet from the trailhead parking area, across Elk Creek. This begins at the Sky Mountain Ranch. This is a high, cascading waterfall that reminds me of the kind of falls one might see in Oregon. (See the chapter on waterfalls.)

 Maps
U.S. Forest Service Bob Marshall, Great Bear, and Scapegoat Complex Map, 2011, USGS Jakie Creek and Double Falls quad maps.

 Contacts
Lewis and Clark National Forest Augusta Information Station (406) 562-3247, Rocky Mountain Ranger District in Choteau (406) 466-5341, Supervisor's office in Great Falls, 791-7700.

Enjoying the top of Steamboat Mountain in spring.

5 Petty Creek/Crown Creek Loop

At the head of Petty Creek looking toward Crown Mountain.

Here's a nice 10-mile loop hike in the Rocky Mountain Front that offers an optional climb and a short side hike to a scenic waterfall—Crown-Ford-Petty Creeks Loop.

It is about a 75-mile drive to the trailhead from Great Falls through Augusta and up the Benchmark Road.

I chose to park at Crown Mountain Trailhead No. 270 and walk back east along the Benchmark Road to the Petty-Ford Trailhead No. 244, a distance of about 1.5 miles. Before you get on trail, take a moment to have a look at the Double Falls, a short distance west of the primitive campground. It is as spectacular a falls as is in the Front.

To begin the hike, cross Ford Creek at the campground. Usually there's a nice log across the creek to make the going easier. The trail starts here and heads uphill, climbing nearly 1,000 feet over the next 1.5 miles to a low saddle above Petty Creek where you'll pass through a wire gate.

Here you'll likely encounter some cattle grazing but also nice views of mountains that were burned by the 1988 Canyon Creek fire and some open grassland before the trail drops into Petty Creek.

At the crossing Trail No. 232 begins, entering heavy forest that opens occasionally as it climbs another 1,000 feet toward Crown Mountain to reveal views of the unnamed mountain south of Crown.

I got off trail at the crossing and decided to explore the hills south of the creek that lead up to that mountain, following elk tracks all the way. I passed through some of the burn and marveled at the regeneration of lodgepole and Douglas fir. I finally emerged from the trees to a cliff high above Petty Creek and views of Crown Mountain. I dropped down to Petty Creek, climbed up and rejoined the trail, walking in forest once again to where the trail met Crown Creek Trail No. 270.

At this point the hiker could peel off, walk up a west-facing ridge to Crown Creek and gain the final 1,400 feet to the top of Crown Mountain.

Instead, I turned down the trail, and within an hour I was back at my car, having enjoyed views of the north face of Crown, Whitewater Creek's waterfalls beneath its face and the Fairview-Sawtooth scenery of the Rocky Mountain Front to the north and east.

The hike took about 5 hours and about 2,000 feet was gained and lost.

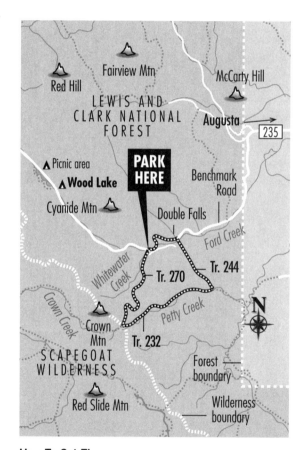

How To Get There

At Augusta, find the Forest Service Benchmark Road that will take you the 20 miles on good gravel to Crown Mountain Trailhead No. 270. Petty-Ford Creek Trail No. 232 is less than a mile east of the Crown Mountain trailhead on the Benchmark Road.

ℹ 5 Petty Creek/Crown Creek Loop

⇄ **Distance**
9 miles and an elevation gain of about 2,300 feet.

④ Difficulty
Moderate to strenuous. About 4 on a scale of 5. The trail rises and falls as it climbs out of Ford Creek, descends to Petty Creek and then climbs to the divide above Crown Creek.

🕐 Time Needed
About 6-8 hours depending on your conditioning.

📅 Best Time
Late spring when the trail is clear of snow to late fall when snow and ice close the Benchmark Road. It is skiable in winter.

🔭 What You'll See
High, above-timberline, alpine country in the heart of the southern part of the Rocky Mountain Front. Along the trail you'll catch glimpses of a waterfall that spills off the mountain into Whitewater Creek.

⚠ Cautions
Grizzly country, steep trail, some trail-finding required because of cattle trails and trampling.

 Sidetrips
Take a few minutes at Petty-Crown Creek and visit Double Falls, just west of the unimproved campground.

 Camping
An unimproved campground at the Petty-Ford Creek trailhead. The Wood Lake campground is only 5 miles from the Crown Mountain trailhead.

📖 Maps
U.S. Forest Service Bob Marshall, Great Bear and Scapegoat Wilderness Complex, 2011. USGS topos: Double Falls, Scapegoat.

📞 Contacts
Lewis and Clark National Forest Augusta Information Station, (406) 562- 3247; Rocky Mountain Ranger District, Choteau, (406) 466-5341; Lewis and Clark National Forest Supervisor's Office, Great Falls, 791-7700.

A log is good enough to cross Ford Creek.

A clearing affords views of surrounding mountains.

Crown Mountain is named for its obvious crown shape.

Crown Mountain (elevation 8,401 feet) is a moderately difficult, but highly satisfying, mountain climb that is mostly on trail.

It is an area you can get to quickly from Great Falls or Helena and offers the excellent alpine scenery in a compact space while attaining over 3,000 feet in elevation.

It is 52 miles to Augusta from Great Falls, and the Crown Mountain trailhead is another 20 miles up the Benchmark Road.

I was there in an hour and a half.

There has been much improvement at the trailhead since last I climbed here. There's a nice parking area, better signs and a clear notion of what's private and what's public.

The 3.5 miles to where Petty Creek Trail No. 232 comes in is mostly in the timber (Douglas fir, whitebark pine and subalpine fir), with an occasional clearing where you can look at Crown Mountain, aptly named because its massive cliffs are crown-shaped. It is a pretty steady pull and about 2,000 feet in elevation gain to that junction.

In one of the clearings you can see a large waterfall on Whitewater Creek, shooting off a cliff at the base of the mountain.

Once you reach the Petty junction, you enter the Scapegoat Wilderness Area and it is above timberline, with stark blond walls of sedimentary rock rising hundreds of feet above you.

Above, a pile of loose rock, the south ridgeline of Crown Mountain opens up like a fan.

This is where you get off the trail and climb. I suggest staying to the right, getting in the scree and begin a 1,000 foot slog up, trying to get to the edge of the cliffs to make the walking easier which would allow you to use your hands if needed.

At about 7,700 feet you can see over the other side, and the views of Steamboat and Haystack Butte mountains are spectacular. Haystack sits like a sentry on the Great Plains.

The higher up you go, the better the views become with the Sawtooth and Teton peaks of the Front coming into view; and when you reach the top, you're able to look all the way across the Bob Marshall and Scapegoat Wilderness Areas. Scapegoat Mountain, with its high-cliff barrier reef, is right in your face.

I was stunned by all of the red-colored mountains in the center of the Bob Mar-

shall and vowed that I would plan trips to climb many of them.

For most climbers I suggest going to the top and coming back down.

However, for the adventuresome and advanced scrambler, there is a way down through Crown Mountain's cliffs to the west. By staying just below those cliffs, I discovered a good animal trail that led me to the ridgeline on the west side of Whitewater Creek.

The ridgeline climbs up and down several small peaks, none requiring more than 700 feet in elevation gain, and staying pretty consistently at about 8,000 feet for more than a mile.

Wood Lake on the Benchmark Road below me came into view, as well as

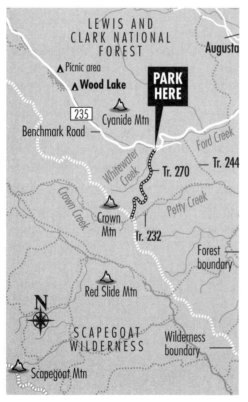

How To Get There

At Augusta find the Forest Service Benchmark Road No. 235 that will take you the 20 miles on good gravel to Crown Mountain Trailhead No. 270.

6 Crown Mountain

 Distance
8 miles and an elevation gain of about 2,700 feet.

Difficulty
Strenuous, close to 5 on a scale of 5. You run out of trail about 600 feet below the summit, and the scramble through the scree adds to its difficulty.

 Time Needed
About 6-8 hours, depending on your conditioning.

 Best Time
Late spring when the trail is clear of snow to late fall when snow and ice close the Benchmark Road.

 What You'll See
High, above-timberline, alpine country in the heart of the southern part of the Rocky Mountain Front. Along the trail you'll catch glimpses of a waterfall that spills off the mountain into Whitewater Creek.

 Cautions
Grizzly country, steep trail, some off-trail scrambling.

 Sidetrips
For the advanced mountain scrambler there is a way down through the west cliffs and ridgeline. There is the possibility of a 10-mile loop going up Crown Creek Trail No. 270 to Petty Crown Trail No. 232 and ending with Petty Ford Creek Trail.

Camping
The Wood Lake campground is only 5 miles from the Crown Mountain trailhead.

Maps
U.S. Forest Service Bob Marshall, Great Bear and Scapegoat Wilderness Complex, 2011. USGS topo: Double Falls, Scapegoat.

Contacts
Lewis and Clark National Forest Augusta Information Station, (406) 562- 3247; Rocky Mountain Ranger District, Choteau, (406) 466-5341; Lewis and Clark National Forest Supervisor's Office, Great Falls, 791- 7700.

Haystack Butte is clearly visible from the top of Crown Mountain.

Alpine Lake, hidden behind limestone folds.

When I hit the trees the traverse became a little more difficult because of rock outcroppings, cliffs and very steep terrain.

However, there were enough openings that I could see my way as the ridge took its twists and turns.

On several of the turns, I could get views of Crown Mountain's north face, and I could make out the faint animal trail I had used.

Once again I saw the waterfall, this time from a different angle, and then it was down to the creek through the timber and up to the trail about a quarter mile from the parking area.

On the trail to Patrol Mountain above Honeymoon Basin.

This is a great hike for older children who will look forward to an objective at the end — a real fire lookout with a ranger who will show them how fires are spotted and handled.

The Benchmark Campground is a nice objective itself, with 32 camping spaces and a hub of trailheads and a major jumping-off point into the Bob Marshall or Scapegoat wilderness areas.

The Patrol Mountain (elevation 8,015 feet) hike begins at Straight Creek, just to the west of the campground.

Follow Trail No. 212 3 relatively flat miles, looking sharp for a trail marker announcing Trail No. 213 that descends through a lodgepole forest to Straight Creek.

Here you'll have to wade this cold, rushing stream. I like to pack light flip-flops or old running shoes I can stash. This stream is wide, but shallow, in mid-summer.

The last 2 miles of the trail are steep (some 30 percent grades), gaining 2,500 feet to the top.

A great place to rest is the aptly named Honeymoon Basin, an open grassy area usually resplendent with wildflowers, just below the Patrol Mountain headwall. This is an ideal spot to take a break and have a snack. You can see where this basin would make the perfect backpack camp. There is a small, but hard-to-find, spring in this basin.

The trail switchbacks up the headwall to the ridge. What follows is a ridge walk to the lookout, manned during the summer fire season and equipped with Forest Service smoke-spotting equipment. In wet years the ridgeline is covered with snow until mid-June.

The most prominent mountain on the horizon is Sugarloaf (elevation 8,698 feet) in the Scapegoat Wilderness Area above the headwaters of the South Fork of the Sun River.

There are good views into the Bob Marshall Wilderness to the north, as well.

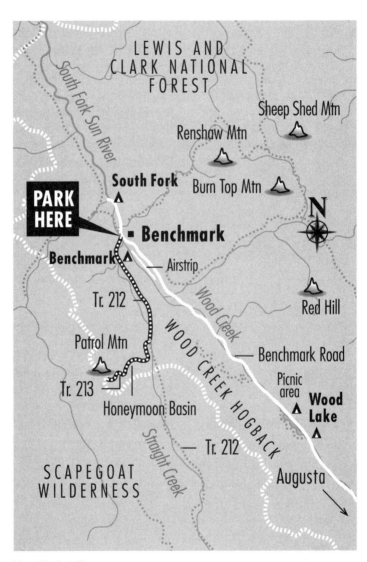

How To Get There

At Augusta take the Benchmark Road 24 miles to the Forest Service's Benchmark campground. At Straight Creek just west of the campground, there is the trailhead for Trail No. 212 that travels the length of Straight Creek south and connects with Trail No. 213 to the top of Patrol Mountain.

7 Patrol Mountain

 Distance
About 10 miles round trip.

 Difficulty
Strenuous. About 4 on a scale of 5, but trail all the way. The last 2 miles of the trail are straight up, gaining nearly 2,500 feet to the summit.

 Time Needed
6-8 hours.

 Best Time
Mid-June to mid-October.

 What You'll See
An active Forest Service lookout staffed during fire season that oversees the north end of the Scapegoat Wilderness and south end of the Bob Marshall Wilderness. This hike is part of the Patrick's Basin Addition to the Scapegoat Wilderness.

 Cautions
This requires wading cold and swift Straight Creek. Take along some sandals or wading shoes you can stash. Some years there is a large snowdrift at the top early in the hiking season.

 Sidetrips
Plan to spend some time on gorgeous Straight Creek. Trails to nearby Renshaw Lake and Pretty Prairie in the Bob Marshall Wilderness Area.

 Camping
Good camping not far from the trailhead in Benchmark Campground.

 Maps
Lewis and Clark National Forest (Rocky Mountain Division) Visitors Map (1988), Bob Marshall, Great Bear and Scapegoat Wilderness Complex map, USGS Benchmark and Wood Lake topo maps.

Contacts
Lewis and Clark National Forest Augusta Information Station, (406) 562- 3247; Rocky Mountain Ranger District, Choteau, (406) 466-5341; Lewis and Clark National Forest Supervisor's Office, Great Falls, 791- 7700.

The Patrol Mountain lookout.

A chilly crossing of Straight Creek on my way to Patrol Mountain.

Renshaw Lake nestled in the trees.

The Rocky Mountain Front is extremely dry country so you wouldn't expect many high country lakes.

That's what makes a place like Renshaw Lake so special.

It is an oasis in a high spot. And it has good fishing, too.

There are a number of very small glacial lakes on the plains outside the Front on the Blackfeet Reservation. These offer good fishing opportunities if you buy a tribal permit as well as your state permit.

There are some outstanding impoundments or reservoirs where streams are dammed up, mainly for irrigation and flood control purposes. Gibson and Swift reservoirs come to mind.

Out on the prairie, but certainly associated with the Front, are reservoirs like Bean Lake, Willow Creek, Eureka and Bynum. These provide plenty of

fishing opportunities as well as camping and some of the best views of the Front one can have from a (short) distance.

As for high country, Our Lake in the South Fork of the Teton country is one of the most visited places on the Front, an alpine lake in a classic cirque with decent fishing and mountain goats.

There are lakes that are off-trail and nearly impossible to find, like little Alpine Lake beneath Wood Creek Hogback and Crown Mountain in the Benchmark county near Wood Lake, an impoundment of Wood Canyon Creek.

The hike to Renshaw Lake provides an opportunity to see one of these rare high lakes and experience a rugged 14.2-mile loop hike or backpack trip in the Front's Benchmark area.

It can be accessed from either the Fairview Trail No. 204 or the Benchmark Creek Trail No. 256; both reached off the Benchmark Road near the backcountry airstrip.

It is roughly 7.5 miles from either starting point to the lake.

I prefer the Benchmark Creek approach because it travels through a canyon of high limestone walls on the flanks of Renshaw Mountain. Trail No. 256 ends about a mile south of the lake cutoff trail, where Trail No. 243, the Lange Creek Trail, comes in on its way to the Patricks Basin north. In less than a mile, where the Fairview-Willow Falls Trail No. 204 intersects No. 243, bear left (or southwest) and walk this trail back to the trailhead at Benchmark Creek, first paralleling Fairview Creek, and then the Benchmark Road.

The Fairview approach is in a bit more timber most of the way, but there are some surprisingly good views of the Burnt Hill ridge to the west and Sheep Shed Mountain ridgeline to the east. Early in the season be prepared for numerous creek crossings on both routes.

Renshaw Lake offers good backpack camping spots accessible to the water.

I have used the lake for a jumping-off point to climb Renshaw Peak, as well.

This is big horse-use country, and I found the trail chewed up in spots and even hammered into widths wide enough to drive two cars on in spots on the Fairview trail.

At the beginning of the Benchmark hike, the trails go off every which way, making it hard to find the right trail. Begin by going through a wire gate; bear right after you pass the Forest Service livestock area. Look for a trail that is within hearing distance of the creek and then crosses the creek after going

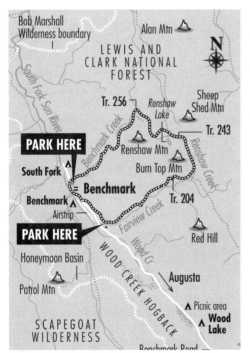

How To Get There

At Augusta, find the Benchmark Road at the southwest end of Main Street. Follow it 32 miles. It is pretty good gravel all the way. Find the trailheads roughly parallel to the end of the backcountry landing strip across the road. Fairview Trail No. 204 can be found at the Benchmark Wilderness Ranch turnout. Benchmark Trailhead No. 256 can be found just beyond the Benchmark Creek bridge. There's also an alternate Trail No. 204 trailhead just before you get to the bridge.

8 Renshaw Lake Loop

 Distance
About 14.2 miles round trip.

 Difficulty
Moderately strenuous, 4 on a scale of 5 with 5 being most strenuous. Steep trails with elevation gain of 3,900 feet and lots of gains and losses on the trail.

 Time Needed
If you're doing this in a day hike, you'll need a minimum of 8 hours.

 Best Time
Mid-June through late fall.

What You'll See
A spectacular limestone canyon hike along the flank of Renshaw Mountain if you take the Benchmark Trail. A lush forest environment if you take the Fairview Trail. The lake is off trail, but there are good paths to it. It is tucked in a draw in the deep forest.

 Cautions
Grizzly country, weather. Finding the proper trail at the Benchmark Creek Trail No. 256 can be difficult because horses have braided the hillside.

Sidetrips
Once you reach the lake, scramble to the west above the lake 1,600 feet to climb Renshaw Mountain (elevation 8,264 feet), which has exceptional views. Renshaw can be reached more easily from the Benchmark Creek trail before it begins its descent to the lake. Another sidetrip is a scramble up Sheep Shed Mountain (elevation 7,629 feet). Find the first good east -running ridge not far from Renshaw Lake and follow it up.

 Camping
Benchmark, 32 sites; South Fork, 7; Wood Lake, 9.

 Maps
Lewis and Clark National Forest (Rocky Mountain Division) Visitors Map (1988), Bob Marshall, Great Bear and Scapegoat Wilderness Complex map, USGS Benchmark, Patricks Basin and Wood Lake topos.

 Contacts
Lewis and Clark National Forest Augusta Information Station, (406) 562-3247; Rocky Mountain Ranger District, Choteau, (406) 466-5341; Lewis and Clark National Forest Supervisor's Office, Great Falls, 791-7700.

through another (possibly open) gate in about a mile from the trailhead.

Many Great Falls folks have enjoyed the hike from Willow Creek Falls on Trail No. 204 to the Benchmark Road. Others have used that trail to get into Lange Creek, which takes you to the heart of the remote Patricks Basin and the head of Gibson Reservoir.

On a high summer day I did this traverse, leaving the Benchmark trail as it began to swing around and drop toward the lake. I got a good view of the lake, some 1,000 feet below and noticed the unnamed mountain (elevation 8,012 feet) just to the south and directly above the lake, climbed it, stopped for some lunch, and then dropped straight down to the lake through the trees and cliffs. Had I stayed on the ridgeline, I could have climbed Burnt Hill (elevation 7,528 feet).

Benchmark Creek Canyon.

Renshaw Lake.

One of the Willow Creek Falls.

Trail No. 204 is full of variety from open prairie to aspen-covered foothills to alpine meadows as it progressively passes a series of waterfalls on a high trail reminiscent of trails found in Glacier or Yellowstone national parks.

The trail begins in open ranch country, weaving its way through open grass and in and out of aspen groves over the first 1.5 miles when it ascends to the flank of Fairview Mountain (elevation 8,264 feet).

It is at this point that the first of 5 waterfalls comes into view.

During the Great Depression, the Civilian Conservation Corps neatly stacked the rocks that shore up this trail.

The first two waterfalls are far enough away and precipitously enough located that you won't be able to reach them. However, they provide great photo opportunities.

The third waterfall is most easy to get to but with a steep scramble down some scree, so be careful. This is an ideal spot for a lunch, although there are other resting spots near cascades above this spot, too.

Continue down the trail through the "notch" between mountains on both sides of the stream and you see way up the broad sloping ramp of Fairview Mountain, which is prominent on the Front skyline seen from Great Falls.

Look back through the notch and Haystack Butte comes into view. The further you travel onto this plateau behind Fairview Mountain, the better you can see it.

The trail continues on to Fairview Creek that ends at the Benchmark Road next to a wilderness airstrip. Trail No. 243 also comes into the trail and continues on into Patricks Basin and ultimately Gibson Reservoir.

Scenic white/yellow limestone peaks rise in all directions around you.

If the hike to the falls isn't enough for you, there's Fairview Mountain, elevation 8,246 feet. Just beyond the falls is a ridge running parallel to the mountain. Ascend it; walk its length to a saddle where you'll find a ridgeline to the top. The higher you get, the better the plains and Haystack Butte to the east come into view.

Or continue on Trail No. 204 past the falls and then the Fairview Plateau and on to Fairview Creek that comes out on the Benchmark Road adjacent to the airstrip, about 11 miles away. You'll be treated to a roadless, backcountry experience along the way, with high, limestone peaks above you in all directions.

Don't forget your camera and a picnic lunch.

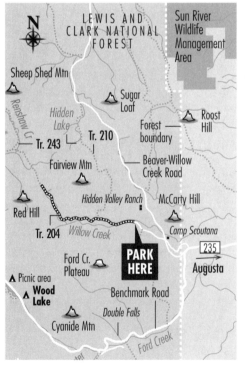

How To Get There

At Augusta, take the Benchmark Road some 15 miles to the Willow-Beaver Creek Road fork. Take the fork to the right and travel about a 1.5 miles to Camp Scoutana. Turn left onto the road. It is a fair two-track road to the trailhead, about 2 miles away. You know you're near when you come to a gate across the road. You can park there, or if you have enough clearance on your car, proceed to another barbed-wire gate where the trail begins.

9 Willow Creek Falls

 Distance
It depends on how far you venture. It is about 3 miles to the Fairview Plateau, where the series of falls finally ends.

 Difficulty
Moderately strenuous with about 1,000 feet in elevation gain. About 3 on a scale of 5 because of elevation gain and distance.

 Time Needed
4-6 hours

 Best Time
As soon as the trail clears in the spring until early winter.

What You'll See
A series of progressively more interesting waterfalls that runs along a narrow canyon on an alpine (Glacier Park-like) trail flanking Fairview Mountain.

Cautions
Grizzly country. High, narrow trail in spots. Considerable horse traffic. Weather, grizzlies, horse encounters, hunters, rocky trail with sharp drop-offs.

 Sidetrips
Progress up the trail deep onto the Fairview Plateau, where it is possible to climb Fairview Mountain (elevation 8,246 feet) from its western face. This area is prime backpacking country. The trail leads to the remote Patricks Basin.

Camping
Home Gulch campground in Sun River Canyon.

 Maps
U.S. Forest Service Bob Marshall, Great Bear, Scapegoat Wilderness Complex, 2011. Lewis and Clark National Forest Rocky Mountain Division Visitors Map. USGS Double Falls, Wood Lake topos.

 Contacts
Lewis and Clark National Forest Augusta Information Station, (406) 562-3247; Rocky Mountain Ranger District, Choteau, (406) 466-5341; Lewis and Clark National Forest Supervisor's Office, Great Falls, 791-7700.

Willow Creek Falls trail.

Another of the Willow Creek Falls.

The Lime Gulch ridge.

This country is easy to miss because the Sawtooth Ridge to the east and the ridge with Fairview Mountain above the Beaver-Willow Creek Road to the west overshadow it. It is timbered on its west face, which makes it even less impressive.

The payoff is the limestone lip on its eastern face that tops off several-hundred-foot stone walls. The views are dominated by Haystack Butte on the plains, Steamboat, Sawtooth and the rocky, unnamed ridge to the west.

I recommend a 3-mile one-way walk up Trail No. 267 to a saddle at the head of Lime Gulch just before it drops over into Cutreef Creek as the trail makes its way in the valley, below the west face of the Sawtooth Ridge.

On one hike to climb Lime Ridge to the east, we happened upon an open south-facing slope of abundant grass that had been frequented by quite a number of elk wintering there.

Begin the hike by driving up the Beaver-Willow Road just beyond the Girl Scout summer camp and looking for a sign announcing the Lime Gulch trail.

We followed the trail up the gulch a few hundred yards and immediately began ascending Lime Ridge through the trees. We reached the ridgeline within 1,000 feet and walking north along the ridge gained an additional 1,100 feet before dropping into the saddle just above the head of Lime Gulch. We walked the trail back through the gulch, dominated by the limestone cliffs above us to the west. As we dropped elevation we could look back at the saddle, dappled with streaks of snow.

The scenery of this area is a combination of Bob Marshall reefs and Glacier Park foothills. If you want to avoid graz-

ing cattle, get there in the spring and
early summer.

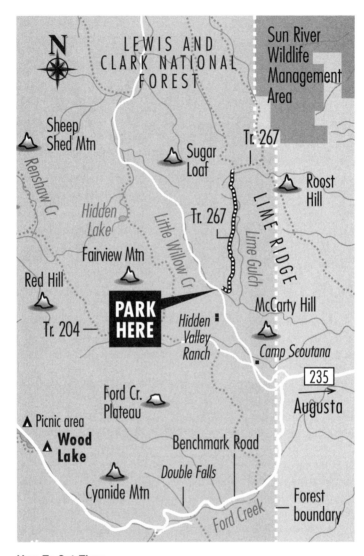

How To Get There

*At Augusta, take the Benchmark Road some 15 miles to the Willow-
Beaver Creek Road fork. Take the fork to the right and travel about
a 1.5 miles to Camp Scoutana. Don't turn into the camp. Continue
on the Willow-Beaver road another 2 miles and start looking for the
Forest Service sign announcing Lime Gulch Trail No. 267 (to the
east).*

10 Lime Gulch

 Distance
7 miles round trip.

 Difficulty
This is a trail that can be walked all the way through to Home Gulch just off the Sun River Canyon, about 15 miles. The hike I recommend is to the saddle above Cutreef Creek, some 3 miles one way. It is a Moderate to Strenuous hike because of the 1,800 feet in elevation gain.

 Time Needed
4-6 hours.

 Best Time
This is four-season hiking country, but the best time is May through November.

 What You'll See
A narrow valley that rises to a saddle between high limestone peaks to the west and low-slung timbered limestone hills to the east. Keep your eyes open because this is great elk country.

Cautions
Grazed in the summer, hunted heavily in the fall. Weather, grizzlies, horse encounters, hunters, rocky trail with sharp drop-offs.

 Sidetrips
Climb the 7,494 foot unnamed peak atop Lime Ridge to the east and get great views of the plains and Haystack Butte to the south. Or continue on Trail No. 267 to Home Gulch, a distance of 13 miles from the beginning of Lime Gulch Trail over moderate terrain.

 Camping
Home Gulch campground in the Sun River Canyon.

 Maps
U.S. Forest Service Bob Marshall, Great Bear, Scapegoat Wilderness Complex, 2011. Lewis and Clark National Forest Rocky Mountain Division Visitors Map. USGS Double Falls, Wood Lake topos.

Contacts
Lewis and Clark National Forest Augusta Information Station, (406) 562- 3247; Rocky Mountain Ranger District, Choteau, (406) 466-5341; Lewis and Clark National Forest Supervisor's Office, Great Falls, 791- 7700.

The Lime Ridge is aptly named for its limestone walls.

Looking down Lime Gulch.

11 Home Gulch/Sun Canyon

Sawtooth Ridge.

The Sun Canyon is the most "civilized" of the Rocky Mountain Front access points.

There are historic dude ranches, the Sun Canyon Lodge resort, trailheads in all directions, Gibson Dam and the Gibson Lake reservoir behind it—all beneath two of the most recognizeable peaks in the Front—Sawtooth (elevation 8,179 feet) although the most accessible and most climbed of the three "teeth" is 8,135 feet and Castle Reef (elevation 8,390 feet).

Yet despite this civlization this is an area where you're most likely to see elk, deer, bighorn sheep and bears, both grizzly and black.

There is no hiking trail representative of the diversity of this area. There are trails around Gibson reservoir and up the gulches which parallel the Sun River on both the north and south sides.

So the question is where to start.

My suggestion is up Home Gulch from the Sun Canyon Resort behind Sawtooth Mountain to Agropyron Flats, so named for the desert wheatgrass that grows there.

Sawtooth is THE major Front mountain visible from Great Falls.

At the flats, limestone reefs rise more than 1,000 feet to the west where you'll spy historic elk migration paths crisscrossing their face.

The Sawtooth (North) climb offers some of the most spectacular, if not the most spectacular, scenery in the Front.

If you climb Sawtooth, Castle Reef, across the Sun River to the north, is a majestic hunk of rock that gets better looking the higher you climb. Gibson Reservoir, which impounds the emerald green waters of the north and south forks of the Sun River, comes into view.

Once you reach the ridgeline, the Great Plains spread out like an ocean at your feet.

On the Sawtooth Ridge there are four "tines" or peaks. I've returned repeatedly to this north hump. The highest point is two more peaks south, 44 feet higher and a little trickier.

The surest way to reach Agropyron Flats and, ultimately, the top of north peak is to start at the Sun Canyon Lodge at Home Gulch, where the owners have always graciously allowed us to park.

There you'll find several horse trails that make the start confusing. I generally cross the creek to the east of the main lodge, ascend a small rise and find a road/horse path that runs south to the base of the mountain. The Forest Service map indicates this is Trail 267. The horse

path just south of the corrals that follows the bottom is the most direct route to the flats.

There are numerous ups and downs, and the trail curves around two major coulees before dumping out onto the Agropyron Flats at Sawtooth Ridge's northwest flank, about 3.5 miles from the car.

Look up and you'll see a number of parallel spines that run down from the top of the mountain.

You'll also be able to view the mountaintop, which is a block with a nipple on top. That's where you'll find the northern cairn.

Once you reach the base of the block, it is a 2,500 foot grunt to the top. Follow the ridgeline up to the cliffs. You can get on the top of the ridge at this point

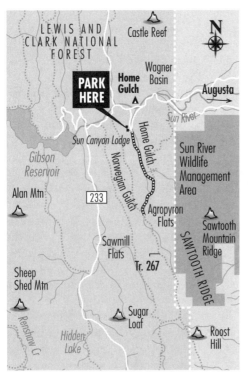

How To Get There

In Augusta, off the main street, take the Sun River Canyon Road. It travels 18 miles to the Lewis and Clark National Forest boundary, where there's a stretch of pavement to the dam. Home Gulch and the Sun Canyon Resort are well marked by a sign. Follow the gulch back past the cabins to the restaurant/ museum. Pick up Trail No. 267 there.

ℹ 11 Home Gulch/Sun Canyon

⇄ Distance
If you go to Agropyron Flats, about 7 miles roundtrip with an elevation gain of about 1,300 feet. To the top of Sawtooth and back, 9 miles.

③ Difficulty
Moderate, a 2.5 on scale of 5, with 5 most difficult. Rated because of distance and some elevation gain. Strenuous if you climb Sawtooth.

🕐 Time Needed
4-5 hours

📅 Best Time
Agropyron Flats can be reached year round, but late spring through hunting season is the best.

👀 What You'll See
It's worth it for the drive alone into the canyon where the emerald Sun River splits the Front. The river is flanked by two of the Front's most handsome mountains: Sawtooth (elevation 8,179 feet) and Castle Reef (elevation 8,390 feet).

⚠ Cautions
Grizzly country. Considerable horse traffic.

🚶 Sidetrips
This is the best way to climb Sawtooth Mountain, which is off trail and accessible from the flats. Another trip is Wagner Basin. Continue up the Road from the Home Gulch turnoff. At the bridge cross the river and start up Hannan Gulch, angling around the south nose of Castle Reef on into the Wagner Basin. Look sharp for the numerous bighorn sheep that frequent the area!

🏕 Camping
Home Gulch campground with 15 spots. Camping and cabins available at the Sun Canyon Lodge. Mortimer Gulch Campground.

📖 Maps
Lewis and Clark National Forest Rocky Mountain Division Visitors Map, Bob Marshall, Great Bear and Scapegoat Wilderness Complex map; USGS Sawtooth Ridge topo.

📞 Contacts
Lewis and Clark National Forest Augusta Information Station, (406) 562- 3247; Rocky Mountain Ranger District, Choteau, (406) 466-5341; Lewis and Clark National Forest Supervisor's Office, Great Falls, 791- 7700.

Below Sawtooth Mountain's north summit.

if you like or follow the base of the cliffs around a bend looking for a crack that will get you on top. You'll have to use your hands to reach the ridgeline through this crack.

Then it is a walk to the top, where the ridge falls off to the east some 1,000 feet and is a tad precarious to the west.

On top you'll be impressed by the size of the other three Sawtooth summits directly in front of you to the south. Be very careful with the footing on the long descent.

Castle Reef Mountain looms over the Wagner Basin in the Sun Canyon Area.

Sawtooth and Castle Reef Mountains are two of the most recognizable named-peaks in the Rocky Mountain Front, visible from Great Falls.

They act as the Sun River Canyon gate posts, flanking both sides of the road west of Augusta that extends to the Gibson Reservoir, a large impoundment of the North and South forks of the Sun River that flow out of the Bob Marshall Wilderness Area.

These mountains thrust skyward, rising more than 3,000 feet from the Great Plains.

But even as they seem unattainable to most there's a highly accessible, kid-friendly basin at their foot that is home to abundant wildlife, myriad wildflowers and views of these two giants that will take your breath away.

It's called Wagner Basin. The length of the trail into it is less than half a mile

(the Forest Service lists it as .44 mile) and provides access to a basin with limitless hiking, climbing, wildlife and wildflower observation.

The basin is bounded by the Sun River that runs an emerald color in the summer and fall. To the north, there's Castle Reef.

"What more could you want of an area?" asked Wayne Phillips, a retired Forest Service ecologist who has led hikes into Wagner Basin for the Montana Native Plant Society and Cascade County Historical Society. "There's lots of botanical diversity, lots of wildflowers. The wetlands are beautiful with beaver dams, and springs. You have a chance of seeing Indian pictographs and big-horn sheep."

He said the area is a National Forest Resource Natural Area which means there is no development there and it is recognized as a special area for research. Therefore, he cautions anyone who enters the area to be, "especially careful not to disturb the site."

He recommends a loop hike that stays between the Sun River and a swamp, circling to the benchland above.

After parking at the designated parking site there's only one way into the basin, heading east along the side of a large limestone wall. The trail is covered in scree, a limestone rock that has fallen from the walls above. It is this wall that if you're observant enough you'll find Indian pictographs. Look, but don't touch these archeological treasures.

For many a highlight of a Wagner Basin trip is the "Skull Tree," just under half a mile from the parking area in a meadow. You'll know it by the picnic table. Spot a good sized limber pine and on its back side are wired about 20 painted white-tail deer skulls, each with a bird painted on it. They're the work of Megan Royce from Dillon, who owns a cabin in nearby Hannan Gulch.

The basin is flanked by and laced with beaver dams.

It is braided with game trails that don't lead anywhere in particular.

The basin is a great place to begin a climb of Castle Reef. A ramp on the mountain's southwest side leads directly to Castle Reef's ridgeline. It is easy to eyeball the unmarked route almost immediately upon entering the basin.

Look to the south and there's mighty Sawtooth Mountain, actually a ridge with several high points. It dominates that horizon.

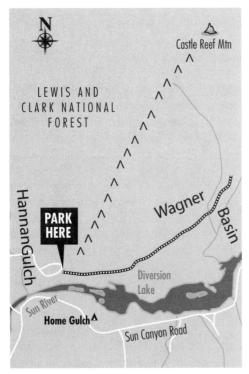

How to Get There

From Augusta, follow the Sun Canyon Road #108 for 18 miles. Turn west onto Hannan Gulch Road #8383, crossing the bridge over the Sun River and travel approximately ¼ mile to the second road heading east on the right. Turn right and continue to the end of the road, passing several summer cabins along the way. Parking is available for several vehicles at the trailhead. No outhouses or other facilities are available.

12 Wagner Basin

Distance
Go as far as you like, but I'd recommend walking at least a mile

Difficulty
This is the easiest hike in the book.

Time Needed
An hour or two

Best Time
This hike can be taken in any season

What You'll See
A variety of high mountain and riparian habitats. Keep a sharp eye for bighorn sheep. There are interesting items such as pictograph drawings on the limestone walls, and a "skull" tree described in the text.

Cautions
Grizzly country

Side Trips
A climb of Castle Reef Mountain or walk the ridge to the east

Campsites
Home Gulch campground with 15 spots. Camping and cabins available at Sun Canyon Lodge. Mortimer Gulch Campground,

Maps
Lewis and Clark National Forest Rocky Mountain Division Visitors Map, Bob Marshall, Great Bear and Scapegoat Wilderness Complex Map; USGS Castle Reef topographical map

Contacts
Lewis and Clark National Forest Augusta Information Station, (406) 562-3247; Rocky Mountain Ranger District, Choteau, (406) 466-5341; Lewis and Clark National Forest Supervisor's Office, Great Falls, 791-7700.

If you don't mind a climb with a little challenge, cross the basin heading east to the prominent limestone ridge that runs to the river. It offers breathtaking views of the entire Sun Canyon area.

This is bighorn country.

In the spring lambs can be seen high on the flanks of Castle Reef. In the fall, the canyon echoes with the sound of rams in rut, exerting their dominance by butting heads.

If Wagner Basin is not enough of a destination, there's plenty to do in the area around it.

There's Home Gulch and the Sun Canyon Lodge directly across the river. The lodge offers outfitting, horseback riding, cabins and camping spots and a full-service restaurant. If you're looking for another outfitter in the canyon try the Triple J.

Josh Carlbom, who owns the lodge, points out that Wagner Basin can be seen by customers eating at the lodge's restaurant. He runs trail rides into the basin.

There is also a Forest Service campground—Home Gulch, with 15 sites.

For many, the Sun River and its Gibson Reservoir are destinations in themselves, offering boating, canoeing, rafting and trout fishing.

Here's how the Lewis and Clark National Forest Web site describes the Wagner Basin hike:

"Wagner Basin Trail is a level, short trail to a large, open flat above Diversion Lake on the North Fork Sun River. The trail is an excellent hike in the fall and spring, when big horn sheep can often be seen frequenting the cliff areas to the north of the flat. Additionally, a variety of wildflowers and native vegetation can be noted along the route. Wagner Flats provide a good place for a picnic, kite flying, or even playing in the river on a summer day. The hike is very short and kid-friendly.

"For the more intrepid hikers, an historical trail which once accessed the north side of the Sun River, before the roads and bridges were built, continues northeast from the meadow into Wagner Basin. The trail is still shown on the Sawtooth Ridge and Castle Reef topographic quads. The tread is not visible in the meadow, but can be found easily to the northeast of the pond, leading up the small creek drainage. The tread is alternately visible and not but experienced hikers can make their way into Wagner Basin and overlook the prairie country from beneath Castle Reef. This route is very steep and not recommended for novice hikers."

13 Mortimer Gulch/Deep Creek

The high mountain country up Mortimer Gulch.

Johnny Mortimer was a mountain-man recluse who lived in the area of the Rocky Mountain Front known as Deep Creek before the turn of the 20th century when the Sun River ran free.

A prominent gulch named for him runs about 5 miles parallel to several others that drain the stark, blond mountain ridges that make up Deep Creek.

Although Mortimer prowled the area more than 100 years ago, he could probably return today and see little change other than what Mother Nature has wrought.

No doubt Mortimer would still be able to live as a hermit, as few people enter Deep Creek except to pass through on the way to the more heavily traveled Bob Marshall Wilderness during the summer or to hunt big game in the fall.

Access is tough here, with the main canyons that spill out onto the Front

blocked by ranches in private ownership.

Long debated as a component of Montana wilderness legislation, some of this area is now part of the Bob.

The 45,000 acre Deep Creek area is bounded on the south by Gibson Reservoir, on the north by the headwall of the South Fork of the Teton River, on the west by the Bob Marshall and on the east by those ranches on the Great Plains.

The area is a wonderful mix of meadows, high mountain peaks and clear, cold, very fast streams.

Access here is by one of a number of gulches.

The route I describe here is north from Gibson Reservoir along Mortimer Gulch, marked by beautiful grass and a nice view of Arsenic Peak.

Trail No. 252 is accessed just before you get to the Mortimer Gulch campground. It proceeds 3 miles gradually uphill on its way to the junction with the Big George cutover Trail No. 259. There are nice views of Grassy Hill and Sawtooth in a number of grassy clearings. Down below you'll also see dude-ranch and summer-home development and the occasional grazing packhorse.

When you've reached the Big George cutover, the trail drops steeply to Big George Creek before doubling back into the gulch where it meets Trail No. 251 that will take you back south along the bottom to Gibson Reservoir. The Forest Service says Big George Creek was named for a man simply known as "Big George," who lived in a cabin at the mouth of the drainage in the late 1800s

and had cut ties for the railroad.

Arsenic Peak (elevation 8,498 feet) dominates the northwestern horizon. Climbing the peak a little north of this junction is not a bad option.

On one grand tour of the Deep Creek I started at Gibson Reservoir up Mortimer Gulch, over to Blacktail, got onto the top of the Cabin Creek trail divide between the Bob Marshall and Deep Creek and then dropped off trail to the South Fork of Deep Creek. I camped here and then spent the next day wandering along the divide above Biggs and South Fork. I used Erosion Creek to take me to the North Fork of Deep Creek and then walked out down the South Fork of Teton Creek trail along

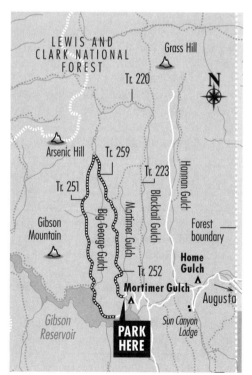

How To Get There

Quickest way in is up Mortimer Gulch. Go to Gibson Dam west of Augusta on Sun Canyon Road No. 208 (27 miles). Just before the Mortimer Gulch campground, there's a trailhead to the north that heads up into the timber.

ℹ️ 13 Mortimer Gulch/Deep Creek

Distance
Eight miles round trip if hiked to its junction with Big George Gulch.

Difficulty
Depends on your distance. Moderate, about a 3 on a scale of 5 because of some elevation gain.

Time Needed
About 4 hours.

Best Time
From late spring through late fall.

What You'll See
A vast variety of Rocky Mountain Front foothills country from timbered forest to open grasslands that offers vistas of mountains such as Grassy Hill and Sawtooth.

Cautions
Outfitters with pack animals use this trail to access the Bob Marshall to the west.

Sidetrips
A good loop is up Mortimer and back down Big George Gulch, about 10 miles.

Camping
Mortimer Gulch Campground (28 campsites) adjacent to Gibson Dam.

Maps
Lewis and Clark National Forest Rocky Mountain Division Visitors Map, Bob Marshall, Great Bear and Scapegoat Wilderness Complex map; USGS Arsenic Peak topo.

Contacts
Lewis and Clark National Forest Augusta Information Station, (406) 562- 3247; Rocky Mountain Ranger District, Choteau, (406) 466-5341; Lewis and Clark National Forest Supervisor's Office, Great Falls, 791- 7700.

the east face of Rocky Mountain peak.

Here's another way to see Deep Creek: Continue up Mortimer Gulch to where it connects to Blacktail Gulch Trail No. 220 (another 2 miles north of the 251-259 junction). Follow that another 2 miles east to the main Blacktail Trail No. 223 and complete the loop back down that trail to Gibson Reservoir, about 6 miles.

Pack horses graze the lower reaches of Mortimer Gulch in the Sun River country.

Mortimer Trail offers grand views of the high country.

Ear Mountain.

There is hardly any more recognizable mountain on the Rocky Mountain Front than Ear Mountain.

It sits out on the Great Plains like an ear turned on its side.

It is a natural magnet for mountain climbers.

If you decide to climb the mountain to its top, I'd recommend you ignore the designated trailhead and instead climb off-trail.

But if you want a trail, the BLM trailhead off the South Fork of the Teton Road has been beautifully developed.

I suggest walking this trail to its end at Yeager Flats, about 2-1/4 miles from the road. What you'll get is a stroll in the Front's foothills marked by open, grassy slopes, aspen groves and breathtaking views of Ear Mountain in front of you.

If you decide to climb this mountain

from here you could find yourself wondering and wandering.

The BLM trailhead points you toward a notch in the mountain's northwest side. Once the notch is attained, you'll pick a game trail that leads you to the southside of the mountain and eventually to the chute to the top.

Unfortunately, the path from Yeager Flats to the notch runs out early and if you aim for this notch you'll be gaining and losing tons of elevation. I've climbed the mountain this way and found the route long and discouraging, although doable.

What I like better is what I refer to as the Little Deep Creek route from the Ear Mountain State Wildlife Management Area parking area off the Bellview Road 22 miles out of Choteau. There's a parking area. Start the climb by following the trace road up the Little Deep

Creek drainage for about 2.25 miles. Leave the trace turning right (north) where the road splits (Y's) and after crossing the first draw, leave the road and head west through the timber to find the ridge and climb the ridgeline from 6,000 feet to about 7,500 feet that brings you to the cliffs. At this point you should be able to see a one-mile game trail across the northeast face of the mountain pointing toward a saddle. At the saddle you should be able to see the back side of the mountain and a terrific game trail in the scree that extends another mile to a breach or 200 foot gully. Scramble up this gully, careful not to kick rocks down on anyone. Then it is an easy stroll to the northwest and the top. The promontory summit to the south of the gully is an easy

scramble. Rountrip: 9.5 miles. Elevation gain: 4,278 feet.

Yet a third route is to begin at the Ear Mountain Game Range parking area on the mountain's east flank, aim for the base of the mountain's cliffs and follow the base to the south side of the mountain. It is a route pioneered by Chris Labunetz of Great Falls, who has also found another way through the cliffs on the southeast flank that requires rope for just one pitch.

The hike begins on a closed road that begins to gain elevation, winding its way toward Ear Mountain.

The nearer you get to the mountain begin looking for the ridge below the sharp cliffs on the southeast corner of the mountain. You can pick it up as you cross the drainage that becomes Little

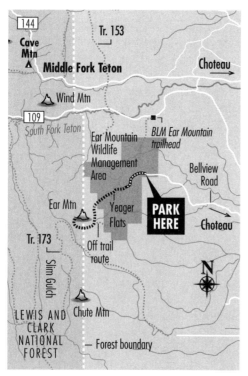

How To Get There

There are two approaches: from the South Fork of the Teton River Road BLM Trailhead and from the Ear Mountain Game Range parking area reached by the Bellview county road outside Choteau.

South Fork approach: Take the Teton River Road 7 miles north of Choteau. It is the same road used to access the Teton Pass Ski Area. At 18 miles begin looking for a Forest Service sign indicating the road to the South Fork of the Teton Road 109. The BLM trailhead is about 2 miles up this road.

Game range approach: Take the Bellview Road 23 miles west out of Choteau to the game range. The road and parking area are well marked.

14 Ear Mountain

 Distance
Elevation gained is 4,278 feet to the top. Distance is about 10-miles roundtrip. It is a 4.3-mile roundtrip to Yeager Flats.

 Difficulty
Easy to moderate if you walk the BLM trail to its end. Strenuous, if you climb to the top of the peak. This is for the serious off-trail hiker who can read a map and follow a line of sight.

 Time Needed
6-8 hours if you climb the peak to the top and come back down. Otherwise, as much time as you need to stroll the well built and marked BLM trail to its end.

 Best Time
Late spring to late fall. The mountain is closed from Dec. 1 to May 15 to protect the wildlife resource.

 What You'll See
Fantastic views of the Rocky Mountain Front and Great Plains; abundant wildlife including bighorn sheep, mountain goats and grizzlies; wildflowers.

Cautions
Getting lost because much of the trip is off-trail. Steep, rocky terrain. No water. Grizzly country.

 Sidetrips
Explore Ear Mountain foothills from either trailhead.

 Camping
Mill Falls Forest Service Campground. There's space to camp on the state Ear Mountain Wildlife Management Area parking site on the mountain's east side.

 Maps
BLM's Choteau map; Lewis and Clark National Forest Visitors Map (Rocky Mountain Division), and Bob Marshall Complex Map. Topographical map:

Ear Mountain. State Department of Fish, Wildlife and Parks Ear Mountain Wildlife Management Area brochure.

Contacts
BLM Great Falls office, 791-7700, state Department of Fish, Wildlife and Parks, Great Falls office, 454-5840, Choteau District of the Lewis and Clark National Forest, (406) 466-5341, Lewis and Clark National Forest supervisor's office, 791-7700.

Deep Creek (about 2 miles into the hike). Follow the drainage up, looking for an opening in the trees on the flank of the ridge. If you can find this opening it is the most direct way up through the grass to the ridgeline. Along the way there are zillions of wildflowers to make some of the pain of the climb more pleasant. It is here that you are most likely to spy bighorns or elk.

At that ridgeline traverse around the mountain at the base of the towering cliffs. As you round the corner Chute Mountain and the unnamed ridges with Rocky Mountain peak behind them come into view. You will gain and lose elevation and there is a pitch of two where you'll have to scramble with your hands and feet.

About half way around the southwest side of the mountain start watching for the scree-chute gap through the cliffs that leads to the top. You'll know you are there when you see a scree opening through the cliffs. There will also be a well-worn footpath coming through the scree from the standard route to the west. It is a scramble through the scree opening, gaining about 200 feet to reach the top. I found that the best way to get through this scree was to follow the wall on my right-hand side. You'll know if you have the wrong opening in the cliffs — you won't be able to get through to the top.

Once on top proceed northwest to the highest point, maked by a geodesic marker proclaiming the peak to have an elevation of 8,580 feet. The top of this mountain is oddly flat for the most part, and tilts east and south. It appears as though you could land a large aircraft on it.

The views from the top display the Rocky Mountain Front from the Scapegoat Wilderness south to Glacier Park on the north, all the way to the snow-covered Swan peaks on the west and the ocean of grass on the Great Plains to the east. There are particularly good views of Old Baldy and Rocky Mountain peaks, the two highest peaks in the Bob Marshall Wilderness at over 9,000 feet high.

On top there is an isolated rock-pile peak reportedly a Native American vision quest site. There are some eerie caves as well that dot the top.

This is one where you can turn around and go back down the way you climbed up. One time a group of us finished the traverse completely around the mountain by following the standard trail back to the northwest notch, finding the base of the cliffs on the north side of the mountain and walking back along the base to the east side of the mountain and back to the trailhead.

The area around the mountain is so beautiful that should you decide you don't want to climb the mountain you haven't wasted the trip.

Great views of Old Baldy from the ridge above Rierdon Gulch.

If there's any valley along the Rocky Mountain Front that reminds me of the scenery from the opening scene from the movie "The Sound of Music," it's the Rierdon Gulch valley.

It's all there: high, above-timberline peaks and grass that crawls up to their base. It is open enough that when you reach a high point you feel like you're Julie Andrews as you swing around taking in the panorama of splendor.

Rierdon Gulch Trail No. 126 can be reached off the South Fork of the Teton Road, the same road to get to the Our Lake or Headquarters Pass trail.

The trail can be a little tricky to find and follow.

It's marked off the road, but as you approach it you realize that to get to it will mean crossing a cold South Fork.

Once across, the trail twists upward toward a ridge away from Rierdon

Creek, which is followed through a forest of lodgepole, Douglas fir and limber pine for more than a mile before switchbacking back to the creek bottom.

The trail, now lined with aspens, climbs out into a beautiful, broad valley with limestone ridges rising on both sides.

It climbs for more than 3 miles out in the open to a high pass above Slim Gulch, which ultimately drops into the North Fork of Deep Creek. This is a great spot for a picnic before turning around for the 4 miles back to the trailhead.

I've seen bighorn sheep and mountain goats from this spot.

I've used the Rierdon Gulch trail as a route into the Deep Creek roadless area further south, a great backpack destination.

Just below the Slim Gulch pass, the

more adventuresome hiker can climb uphill off trail to the east, gaining the ridgeline about 400 feet above.

The views from this point are stupendous with Rocky Mountain Peak, the highest point in the Bob Marshall Wilderness Area at 9,392 feet, dominating the western view. Ear Mountain commands the view to the east.

For the truly strong hiker, there's the 14.25-mile Rierdon-Green Gulch loop, which follows Rierdon to Slim Gulch down to the North Fork of Deep Creek

Trail No. 135 that connects to Trail No. 127 that follows Sheep Gulch back to Green Gulch. It is about a mile back along the South Fork Road to the Rierdon Gulch trailhead.

This hike circumnavigates the high, unnamed peak that separates Green and Rierdon Gulches.

North Fork Trail No. 135 serves as a cut-across trail that is a sort of crossroads in this Rocky Mountain Front roadless area of towering peaks and limestone canyons.

How To Get There

You'll start with the Teton River Road 7 miles north of Choteau. It is the same road used to access the Teton Pass Ski Area. It is paved much of the way. At 18 miles begin looking for a Forest Service sign indicating the road to the South Fork of the Teton Road 109, which you'll follow 8 miles to the trailhead for Rierdon Gulch Trail No. 126. You'll have to cross the South Fork to begin this hike. Once across the creek bear right (west), and you should start picking up stones marking the trail that crosses this wash. The trail heads up more steeply as you climb out of the bottom.

ℹ 15 Rierdon/Green Gulch Loop

⇄ **Distance**
It is about 4 miles to the head of Rierdon Gulch. The full loop is 14.25 miles.

⑤ Difficulty
Strenuous because of trail-finding, creek crossings and elevation gain and loss.

🕐 **Time Needed**
About 6 to 8 hours.

Best Time
After the snow clears.

What You'll See
"Sound of Music" alpine scenery at the head of Rierdon Creek. Keep an eye out for bighorn sheep and mountain goats as well. If you hike to Slim or Sheep gulches you will be in the Deep Creek Addition to the Bob Marshall Wilderness.

⚠ Cautions
Grizzly habitat, trail-finding can be touchy.

Sidetrips
If you reach the head of the gulch before it drops over into Slim Gulch, climb the 250-500 feet to the top of the ridge to the east. It offers spectacular views of Rocky Mountain Peak and the high country above the gulch. If you're really ambitious, continue down Slim Gulch to the North Fork of Deep Creek then back to Sheep/Green gulches for a 14.25-mile loop hike.

Camping
Mill Falls, 4 campsites.

Maps
Lewis and Clark National Forest Visitors Map, Rocky Mountain Division, (1988), Bob Marshall, Great Bear and Scapegoat Wilderness Complex Map, USGS Ear Mountain topo, BLM's Choteau map.

📞 **Contacts**
Rocky Mountain Ranger District, Choteau, (406) 466-5341; Lewis and Clark National Forest Supervisor's Office, Great Falls, 791-7700.

It's possible to mountain bike Rierdon Gulch.

The folded landscape of the Front are on display in Rierdon Gulch.

Headquarters Pass.

The hike along Trail No. 165 to Headquarters Pass is among the most satisfying treks on the Front.

It is a main thoroughfare into the Bob Marshall Wilderness and the North Fork of the Sun River.

It follows one of the forks of the South Fork of the Teton River from its source to a high pass at the flank of Rocky Mountain peak, at 9,392 feet, the highest point in the Bob.

Along the way hikers are treated to a variety of sights from deep forest to alpine plateau.

Pick up the trail just north of the parking lot. It travels through deep forest. Stop and read the Forest Service interpretive signs explaining the kinds of animals you may see and the kind of forest you're traveling through. In early summer look for beargrass.

In about a half mile the Our Lake Trail No. 184 breaks off to the north.

Continue straight ahead and you'll begin to climb above the stream.

The ridgeline to the south climaxes into Rocky Mountain peak.

In about a mile and a half, the trail starts to switchback up the mountain, and thin waterfalls come into view.

Above the waterfalls the trail spills out into an open area beneath Rocky Mountain peak.

The basin is littered with white limestone boulders.

Look sharp, because one of these could be a mountain goat, which frequent the area and use a clear, cold spring just off the trail, which is the water source for the falls you've just passed.

It is here that you can see the off-trail ridge that many use to scramble up Rocky Mountain peak.

From here the trail switchbacks to the pass where you'll be treated to the Bob Marshall Wilderness Area sign—a real photo op!

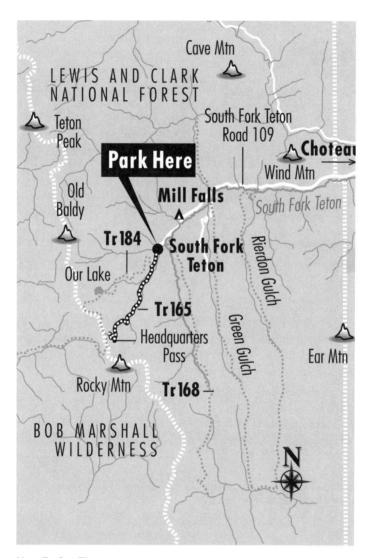

How To Get There

Take the Teton River Road 5 miles north of Choteau. It is the same road used to access the Teton Pass Ski Area. It is paved much of the way. At 18 miles, begin looking for a Forest Service sign indicating the road to the South Fork of the Teton Road 109, which you'll follow to its end, about 11 more miles. This parking lot serves the trail to both Headquarters Pass and Our Lake.

16 Headquarters Pass

 Distance
About 7 miles round trip.

 Difficulty
Moderate to More Difficult, about a 3.5 on a scale of 5, with 5 being most difficult. I've rated it this way because there is a steady elevation gain, climbing 2,141 feet.

 Time Needed
About 5-6 hours.

 What You'll See
Waterfalls, views of the highest peak in the Bob Marshall Wilderness, Rocky Mountain peak (elevation 9,392 feet). At the pass you'll look into the Bob Marshall itself. Mountain goats frequent this trail. Some of this hike is part of the Our Lake Addition to the Bob Marshall Wilderness.

 Best Time
Early June until snow blows the South Fork road closed in late November.

 Cautions
Grizzly country.

 Sidetrips
The experienced mountain climber will want to use this trail to climb Rocky Mountain Peak from a western ridge or the pass itself. There is a way to get to Our Lake from the pass by attaining the saddle just west of the ridgeline running north from the pass and then dropping steeply to the lake. The South Fork Trail No. 168 is a scenic walk along Rocky Mountain Peak's east flank.

 Camping
Mill Falls, 4 campsites.

 Maps
Lewis and Clark National Forest Visitors Map, Rocky Mountain Division, (1988), Bob Marshall, Great Bear and Scapegoat Wilderness Complex Map, USGS Our Lake topo.

Contacts
Rocky Mountain Ranger District, Choteau, (406) 466-5341; Lewis and Clark National Forest Supervisor's Office, Great Falls, 791-7700.

Horses are regular travelers across the pass.

Arriving at Our Lake, a tranquil sight.

Our Lake (also known as Hidden Lake on some maps) is the first introduction to the Rocky Mountain Front for many hikers.

It is short enough that it makes a quick day hike, and while 1,500 feet is gained, it is not so strenuous that most healthy people can't do it if they pace themselves.

Pick up the trail just north of the parking lot. It travels through deep forest. Stop and read the Forest Service interpretive signs explaining the kinds of animals you may see and the kind of forest you're traveling through. In early summer look for beargrass.

In about a half mile the Our Lake Trail No. 184 breaks off to the north.

Follow it as it switchbacks up a hillside where the trail meets the small fork of the South Fork of the Teton River, which drains the lake. There are occasional vistas as the trail works its way back and forth. When the trail flattens out, a waterfall and the ridgeline come into view.

Years ago the Forest Service made a wise decision to disallow camping at Our Lake because of pollution and congestion problems.

The Forest Service put in a pit toilet at the base of the headwall below the lake and has restricted backpackers to this spot.

In late spring and early summer, the last half mile of walking up this headwall can be in deep snow.

Once the snow has cleared, however, hikers follow a switchback trail to the lake.

Keep your eyes sharp because mountain goats are frequent visitors to the lake.

The lake contains small cutthroat trout, which can be finicky and difficult to reach without a spinning outfit.

People have cut a trail around the lake. Try a hike to the saddle above the lake that looks down into Ray Creek in the Bob Marshall Wilderness Area.

Hearty scramblers who don't mind going off trail will be tempted to take the first gully on the south they encounter for a traverse to Headquarters Pass. In early summer there is often a snow-drift here. The first several hundred feet of elevation gain can be a little tricky because it is steep. Above the gully, head for the saddle to the west and then down east and south to reach the pass.

Don't be surprised to see crowds of hikers at the lake.

If you want it to yourself, go midweek or save this for a fall trip.

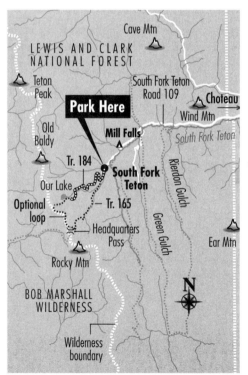

How To Get There

Take the Teton River Road 7 miles north of Choteau. It is the same road used to access the Teton Pass Ski Area. It is paved much of the way. At 18 miles begin looking for a Forest Service sign for the South Fork of the Teton Road 109, which you'll follow to its end, about 11 more miles. This parking lot serves the trail to both Headquarters Pass and Our Lake.

17 Our Lake

 Distance
About 5 miles round trip.

 Difficulty
Moderately strenuous. About a 3.5 on a scale of 5, with 5 being the most strenuous. The difficulty indicates an elevation gain of 1,500 feet

 Time Needed
5-6 hours

 Best Time
Early June until snow blows the South Fork road closed in late November.

 What You'll See
An alpine lake in a high mountain cirque. Most of this area is now part of the Our Lake Addition to the Bob Marshall Wilderness.

 Cautions
Grizzly country.

 Sidetrips
It is possible to traverse to Headquarters Pass and make a loop hike out of this. At the lake, ascend the first gully in sight to your left (southwest) angling slightly west toward a saddle. Climb to the top of the ridge and descend to the pass by proceeding gradually east and south.

 Camping
Mill Falls, 4 campsites.

 Maps
Lewis and Clark National Forest Visitors Map, Rocky Mountain Division, (1988), Bob Marshall, Great Bear and Scapegoat Wilderness Complex Map, USGS Our Lake topo.

 Contacts
Rocky Mountain Ranger District, Choteau, (406) 466-5341; Lewis and Clark National Forest Supervisor's Office, Great Falls, 791-7700.

A waterfall drains Our Lake.

Our Lake as viewed from a saddle between the lake and Headquarters Pass.

Rocky Mountain Peak's north face.

It is always a bragging point to have climbed the highest mountain peak in a particular range. That's because it usually involves a feat of endurance and skill.

If you are in pretty good shape and comfortable scrambling off trail, Rocky Mountain Peak in the Rocky Mountain Front is a relatively easy "highest" peak to conquer. It's also the highest point in the Bob Marshall Wilderness at 9,392 feet.

The route I suggest is mostly on trail and takes you to one of the "must see" places in the Front—Headquarters Pass.

Take the Headquarters Pass Trail No. 165 from the South Fork of the Teton River parking lot. The trail is well-marked, but where it meets the Our Lake Trail, make sure to bear left and stay on the Headquarters Pass Trail. The trail climbs steadily through the forest

and then past a series of waterfalls and then to the great basin beneath Rocky Mountain Peak, where there is a spring frequented by mountain goats. The trail snakes from here up the hillside to the west and the pass.

Stand at the bottom in this basin and you'll see a logical route to the top via a north ridge that arises from the basin. This is an easy way down. I don't suggest it as a route up for the first climb because it involves a lot of scree crawling.

Instead, climb to Headquarters Pass on the trail. Stop and enjoy views across the Bob Marshall Wilderness Area to the Chinese Wall. Then look directly south and up (to your left facing west) and you'll see a high saddle.

Drop down the trail a few hundred yards and start walking up to this saddle. It is a slog but only about 500 feet of elevation gain. At the saddle it is a scramble up the ridgeline to the west to the top. There are a couple of points where you'll have to use your hands as well as your feet, but there is no serious exposure at any point.

On top you'll feel like you are on the roof of the world. It is spectacular in every direction. Your eyes will be filled with views of the entire Bob Marshall Wilderness complex, including the Great Bear and Scapegoat wilderness areas. You'll see all the way to the Swan Range and across the Sun River watershed to the west, with the Chinese Wall, Pentagon, Holland, Swan and Silvertip peaks all in view. To the south is the Scapegoat, to the north the Great Bear and the southern peaks of Glacier including the St. Nick spire and mighty Mount Stimson. The Great Plains are east beyond the Rocky Mountain Front with the Sweetgrass Hills, the Highwoods, Belts and various buttes interrupting the vistas.

After enjoying the views, you can come down the way you went up, and then back down the Headquarters Pass Trail, or you might want to consider joining up with the trail by descending to the east and down a north ridge back to the basin, also a pretty good "up" route.

I've taken a number of first-time mountain climbers on this hike with great success.

It is well worth the effort.

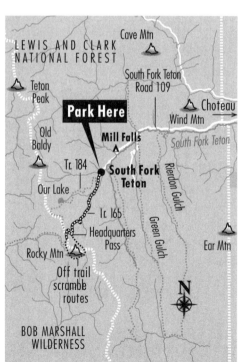

How To Get There

Take the Teton River Road 7 miles north of Choteau. It is the same road used to access the Teton Pass Ski Area. It is paved much of the way. At 18 miles, begin looking for a Forest Service sign indicating the road to the South Fork of the Teton Road 109, which you'll follow to its end, about 11 more miles. This parking lot also serves the trail to both Headquarters Pass and Our Lake.

Old Man of the Hills Mountain west of Dupuyer.

Wagner Basin is a National Forest Resource Natural Area and the easiest hike in this book.

Mountain Douglasia alpine wildflowers dot the limestone ridge near Teton Pass in West Fork Addition to the Bob Marshall Wilderness.

The Sun River splits a large limestone wall, creating the Sun River Canyon.

An aerial view of the Choteau Mountain area.

Crown Mountain's north face.

The ridge line leading to Scarface Mountain in the Badger-Two Medicine Area.

A backpack camp below Rocky Mountain Peak,
the highest point in the Bob Marshall Wilderness.

*After the 2007 fire near Mount Wright,
the Mountain Hollyhock wildflower moved in.*

*The south end of Walling Reef as seen from the top of
Old Man of the Hills Mountain west of Dupuyer.*

Climbing the animal trail on the south face of Ear Mountain west of Choteau.

This mountain goat billy guards Headquarters Pass.

In the Patrick's Basin Addition to the Bob Marshall Wilderness.

This alpine lake jewel hangs in a cirque below Wood Creek Ridge in an off-trail basin above the Benchmark Road west of Augusta.

An eroded outcropping on the Castle Reef Mountain ridge leaves windows for viewing the Sun River Canyon below.

18 Rocky Mountain Peak

 Distance
About 8.5 miles round trip

 Difficulty
Strenuous. Elevation gain of 4,431 feet.

 Time Needed
About 8 hours

 Best Time
Between May and November when the area is free of snow.

 What You'll See
Magnificent views of the Rocky Mountain Front, Bob Marshall, Scapegoat and Great Bear wilderness areas, portions of Glacier National Park and the Great Plains as far as the Sweetgrass Hills. The climb is in the Our Lake Addition to the Bob Marshall Wilderness.

 Cautions
Only 3 miles of the hike is on trail. That means you'll be scrambling on rock and scree, off-trail in high elevations. Grizzly country. Changeable weather, possibly lightning on ridgetop.

 Sidetrips
After climbing the peak, return to Headquarters Pass where it is possible to traverse to Our Lake and back to the parking lot. No trail.

 Camping
Mill Falls Campground or at the primitive camping at trailhead.

 Maps
U.S. Forest Service Bob Marshall, Great Bear and Scapegoat Wilderness Map, 2011; USGS Our Lake topo map. Choteau Mountain BLM map.

 Contacts
Rocky Mountain Ranger District of Lewis and Clark National Forest in Choteau, (406) 466-5341, Lewis and Clark Forest Headquarters, Great Falls, 791-7700.

Scrambling the north facing ridge to Rocky Mountain Peak is challenging.

Along the east face of the Rocky Mountain Front between Clary Coulee and Blackleaf Canyon.

You might call this hike the "Grand Tour" of the Front.

It covers more than 12 miles of the most striking scenery in the Front, showing off isolated high peaks, yet also revealing evidence of natural-gas development.

This is a strenuous hike that requires some route finding, because the Forest Service's most detailed map is wrong (Bob Marshall, Great Bear and Scapegoat Wilderness Complex map, 1990) where Clary Coulee Trail No. 177 meets the Pamburn Creek Trail No. 153.

This is also a hike that you might want to consider doing with two parties that would start at either end and pass keys in the middle because it is a long walk-through.

I've hiked it both ways and prefer starting at the Blackleaf Canyon Trail No. 106.

Walk through that glorious limestone canyon, break out in the open and within a mile there is a trail sign indicating the cut-across trail to the south, Trail No. 153 that goes all the way back to the Teton Canyon Road via Pamburn Creek, some 12 miles away by way of the Blindhorse Outstanding Area.

The hike I'll describe cuts away at Blindhorse and with some careful off-trail route-finding west goes up a dry waterfall to the Clary Coulee Trail No. 177. I favor this route over Pamburn because it hugs the bottom of Choteau Mountain, a long ridge of limestone. Pamburn is open to livestock grazing and after Blindhorse stays in the forest where the views aren't as open or majestic as the Clary Coulee route. The first couple of miles cross private land, and permission to cross should be sought.

You cross Blackleaf Creek south to

reach Trail No. 153 that climbs immediately and crosses the flank of Mount Werner (elevation 8,090 feet). I've used this route to climb this triple-peaked mountain. The trail is also the headwaters of Muddy Creek where you'll find remnants of old natural gas well development. There are capped wells and rusted-out steam engines lying on their sides here. Hunters' camps litter this area as well.

After hiking through dense timber with occasional views of Mount Werner, you will see unnamed mountains to the south come into view, including a large unnamed blocky mountain, before the trail breaks out into the grass in front of it and a low saddle. It then drops down into a broad alpine valley where the forks of Blindhorse Creek originate.

The base of this high valley is the half way point of the hike where it gets tricky.

Notice that the unnamed peak that (we've unofficially named Guthrie Peak) has a couple of (usually dry) waterfall beds coming off its east face.

Choose the one to the south and proceed up it.

It rises more than 100 feet and is steep. However, the handholds are good and footing stable. Mountaineers call this Class 3 climbing. Stay in the rock

How To Get There

*Option 1 (Blackleaf to Clary Coulee north to south route):
About 85 miles northwest of Great Falls. Drive to Bynum. Take a good gravel county road some 15 miles west of Bynum to the canyon. There is a good parking area at the mouth of the canyon where the road ends. Trail No. 106 that connects to Trail No. 153 begins here.*

Option 2 (Clary Coulee to Blackleaf south to north route): Take the Teton River Road that parallels the Teton River some 7 miles north of Choteau. At about 15 miles the road turns from pavement to gravel. At that point it's another 7 miles to the clearly marked Clary Coulee Trail No. 177 to the north.

Option 3 (Pamburn Creek to Blackleaf Canyon): This is the Trail No. 153 route all the way. It parallels Clary Coulee but is several hundred feet below it. At mile 25 on Teton Road.

19 Clary to Blackleaf

 Distance
12 miles

 **Difficulty**
Strenuous. 4.5 on a scale
of 5, with 5 the hardest.
Serious route finding,
distance and 3,500 feet
elevation gain and loss.

Time Needed
6-8 hours

Best Time
Early summer until snow in
the fall.

What You'll See
We call this the "Grand
Tour" of the Front because
it offers some of the best
scenery of this special area.

Cautions
Grazing, a trail that shows
on the map but doesn't
exist.

Sidetrips
Explore the Blindhorse
Outstanding Management
Area

Camping
If you start at Clary Coulee
or Pamburn Creek, there's
nearby Cave Mountain
Campground at the mouth
of the Middle Fork of Teton
River. The Blindhorse is
prime backpacking country.
If you start at Blackleaf,
camping is possible at
the trailhead. There are
several undesignated and
undeveloped areas just east
of the trailhead.

Maps
Lewis and Clark National
Forest Visitors Map (1988),
Bob Marshall, Great Bear
and Scapegoat Wilderness
Complex Map, BLM's
Choteau Mountain map,
USGS Cave Mountain and
Volcano Reef topo maps.

Contacts
Lewis and Clark National
Forest in Great Falls, 791-
7700, Rocky Mountain
Ranger District, Choteau,
(406) 466 5341. BLM
office in Great Falls, 791-
7700, Lewistown office,
(406) 538-7461.

bottom as it hooks to the south and begin looking for a distinct trail that enters the thick timber.

If you find this, you're on Trail No. 177 that climbs and falls along the face of Choteau Mountain all the way back to Clary Coulee.

Here's another way to hook up 153 and 177. Gene Sentz describes the link between Trails No. 177 and No. 153:

"On your map, find Section 18, T25N, R8W, and you'll see where the Chicken Coulee trail comes up from the east to hook into 153. If you keep poking around pretty much due west up that draw (just on the north side), you'll eventually find an old trail. We ride it horseback. It's about 3 miles south of where the nonexistent trail is shown on the USFS map.

Remains of old development at head of Muddy Creek.

"If you're coming up Pamburn Creek on 153 from the south, as soon as you go through the gate at the very head of Pamburn and start dropping north down into Chicken Coulee, bear to the west and cross the draw (to the north side) and you'll find that old trail.

"There are a few other places farther north where you can bushwhack or climb between the two trails, and I've done it on foot …, but it's steep and no trails."

Once you've reached 177, the walk is a glorious up-and-down stroll across the drainages that pour off Choteau Mountain. You'll see ways to climb this glorious limestone chunk of rock as you pass beneath it.

Keep an eye open for the bighorn sheep and mountain goats that frequent its flanks.

About the only problem you may encounter is a number of trails that braid the grasslands. They eventually connect on an open bench.

Backpackers rest at Route Creek Pass.

This is an area you'll share with the dudes from the 7 Lazy P Guest Ranch that is headquartered on the creek.

But their enjoyment will enhance your experience when you encounter them on the trail.

The hike to Route Creek Pass (elevation 7,263 feet, a gain from the trailhead of about 2,265 feet), has a little bit of everything to interest you.

The beavers have worked the bottoms pretty hard. You'll notice that traveling up the Teton Road to reach the trailhead. I've seen moose droppings on the trail near here, but haven't seen the moose yet.

The Middle Fork travels in a narrow little valley, hemmed in on each side by towering limestone peaks and cliffs. The trail climbs from heavy forest to the Middle Fork's headwaters at the base of Old Baldy Mountain.

Trail No. 108 begins not far from the secluded campground at a good parking lot, and cuts its way through aspen thickets.

Within a mile look for the Lonesome Ridge Trail No. 154 that crosses the Middle Fork and climbs to the south and a saddle that drops to the South Fork of the Teton River Road through dense forest. Have a car waiting on the road for a nice point-to-point walk.

Cave Mountain is also climbable about a mile from the trailhead.

At about 4 miles into this hike you'll get good views of the Middle Fork waterfall.

The Route Creek headwall is at the end of the valley and the trail winds back into the forest as each drainage comes down from Cave Mountain to the north.

Along the way are open hillsides of grass for scenery and wildflowers, great open areas for rests and picnics, and of course the pass itself has all of the above. Don't forget to keep your eyes open for the mountain goats that frequent these high places.

The views from Route Creek Pass are down into the Sun River country, some of which burned in recent years. Wapiti Peak in the Bob comes into view.

I've climbed Old Baldy to the south from here and Teton Peak (elevation 8,416 feet) to the north.

Both are more easily climbed from other aspects, but Old Baldy is very satisfying from this side.

Hiking back reveals good views of Cave Mountain to the west and Choteau Mountain to the north.

This country is particularly scenic in the fall with the aspen in full color.

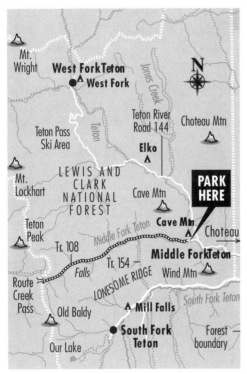

How To Get There
Choteau to Cave Mountain campground turnoff on the Teton River Road off U.S. 89. Drive across the bridge, past the campground to a parking area where you'll find Trail No. 108 into Route Creek Pass.

ℹ️ 20 Route Creek Pass/Middle Fork Teton

 Distance
10.6 miles round trip

 Difficulty
3.5 Moderate, 3.5 on a scale of
5 with 5 the most difficult.
Elevation gain of 2,265 feet
and distance.

 Time Needed
6-8 hours

 Best Time
Late spring through late fall.

 What You'll See
This is a narrow valley that
follows the Middle Fork of
the Teton River to its source,
gaining about 2,000 feet
to a high mountain pass
and into the Bob Marshall
Wilderness Area's Sun River
country. The trail traverses
a forested river bottom to its
alpine conclusion at the foot
of Old Baldy Peak (elevation
9,156 feet), one of the
highest points in the Bob.

 Cautions
Horse traffic, grizzly country.

 Sidetrips
From Route Creek Pass
climb Old Baldy's sharp
north ridge some 1,400 feet
to the top. Another good
sidetrip is to Lonesome
Ridge Pass, (about 2 miles);
climb on Trail No. 154 from

the Middle Fork through the
forest to a high, grassy saddle above the South Fork of
Teton River Road. For those
who like off-trail scrambles,
Middle Fork Trail No. 108 is
about the best access point
for Cave Mountain (elevation
7,542 feet), about a mile
up the trail. (See chapter on
mountain climbing.)

 Camping
Elko with 3 campsites. Cave
Mountain, 14 campsites.
West Fork, 6 campsites.

 Cross Country Skiing
Excellent place to ski
when there's good snow.
Good connecting ski to the
Lonesome Ridge and down
the South Fork of the Teton.

 Maps
Lewis and Clark National
Forest Visitors Map, Rocky
Mountain Division, (1988),
Bob Marshall, Great Bear
and Scapegoat Wilderness
Complex Map, USGS Our
Lake topo. BLM Choteau
map.

 Contacts
Rocky Mountain Ranger
District, Choteau, (406)
466-5341; Lewis and Clark
National Forest Supervisor's
Office, Great Falls, 791-7700.

A falls on the Middle Fork Teton along the trail.

The dynamic peaks of the Jones Creek valley.

This long-broad valley has some of the best scenery on the Rocky Mountain Front available with little effort.

Trail No. 155 is on a long valley floor behind the massive, naked west flank of Choteau Mountain and several unnamed 8,000 foot bald peaks to its north. On the west is an unnamed limestone ridge of mountains reachable by the West Fork of Jones Creek Trail No. 156. Far to the north is the headwall of Mount Werner, which presides over Blackleaf Canyon.

I've used these trails to climb both Choteau and the West Fork ridgeline, in addition to the peaks adjacent to Choteau.

Choteau and the other peaks to the east are reached by ramp-like ridges that rise from the Jones Creek valley. It's a matter of identifying them and following these ramps up.

The West Fork ridge is a little trickier but amounts to following Trail No. 156 as far as it will go and scrambling to the top of the ridge. Trail 156 comes in just under 2 miles up the main trail and is a good turnaround point.

Once while hiking No. 156 to the ridgeline, I got a startling surprise to see a grizzly sitting on an adjacent high point on the ridge, not too far away. This West Fork ridge looms above the Teton River canyon more than 1,000 feet below.

The Jones Creek valley has been worked over by hard flooding, fire, beavers, livestock and logging.

If you have difficulty finding the trail or lose it, the object is to stay on the floor of the creek bottom where it is open and flat.

Start the trip just off the Teton Canyon Road at an unmarked, but much-used, camp area in the aspens. You'll have to cross a small stream that has been worked by beavers at the beginning, but it doesn't amount to much, and there is a wooden board across it to assist you.

The trail weaves through aspen groves until it breaks out into the open, revealing the high, bare backside of Choteau Mountain and her unnamed sisters.

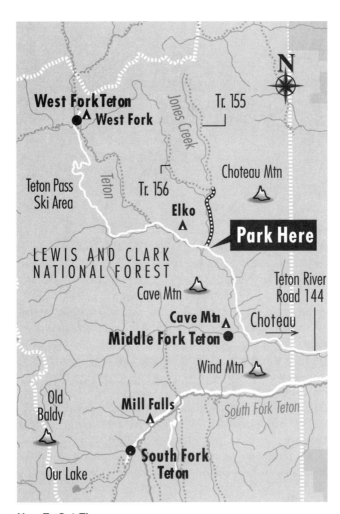

How To Get There

Seven miles north of Choteau turn onto the Teton River county road that leads to the Teton Pass Ski Area. The well marked Jones Creek trail No. 155 is 2 miles beyond the Cave Mountain Forest Service campground.

21 Jones Creek

 Distance
This will be an up-and-back hike. One logical turnaround is where the West Fork Trail No. 156 comes in, just under 2 miles from the trailhead.

 Difficulty
Easy. 2 on a scale of 5, with 5 being most difficult. There is very little elevation gain along the bottom. The difficulty rises with the distance hiked.

 Time Needed
Depends on distance. If you hike as far as Trail No. 156, 3-5 hours.

Best Time
Early spring to late fall, although it can be skied in a good winter if the wind hasn't hammered it too hard.

 What You'll See
This is easy terrain with little elevation gain. It has some of the best scenery in the Rocky Mountain Front. The trip traverses a trail in a broad creek wash between massive Choteau Mountain to the east and an unnamed ridge to the west.

 Cautions
Weather, grizzly country, water.

 Sidetrips
Trail No. 156 up the West Fork of Jones Creek. Choteau Mountain climb (elevation 8,398 feet).

 Camping
Cave Mountain campground is nearby. Good primitive camping available near the trailhead.

 Cross Country Skiing
When there is enough snow, this is a good place to ski, although windy much of the time.

 Maps
U.S. Forest Service's Bob Marshall, Great Bear, and Scapegoat Wilderness Complex map, 2011; USGS Cave Mountain topographic quadrangle.

Contacts
Rocky Mountain Ranger District, Choteau, (406) 466-5341; or Lewis and Clark National Forest Supervisor's office, 791-7700.

One of the many North Fork Teton crossings.

22 North Fork Teton River Canyon

Hikers cross and recross the Teton River.

Save this hike for a blistering hot day when you don't mind getting wet.

This can be a walk through or point-to-point hike if you have two cars or an out-and-back hike if you don't.

If you walk all the way through, be aware that you should wear waterproof sandals or shoes because you'll be in the creek quite a bit crossing back and forth.

Don't let the cold, rushing water stop you. Except for the spring melt, it is hardly knee deep but can be frightfully cold.

The advantage to pushing on is that going in either direction the farther you go, the more towering the limestone cliffs become as they shoot into the sky above you.

Anywhere along the creek is a magnificent picnic spot.

Look sharp and you'll find great swimming (or fishing holes), too.

If you begin from the Teton Road, you're just above where Waldron Creek comes pouring into the stream, not a bad spot to check the fishing.

The first mile or so goes through the forest above inviting table rocks in the creek, climbing and eventually dropping within a mile to your first crossing, where the jumbled talus of the limestone walls drops into the Teton.

From here the trail follows the tight canyon and the bottom, forcing numerous stream crossings over the next 2 miles until you come out on the flat near the West Fork cabin and get great views of Mount Wright on the northwest horizon.

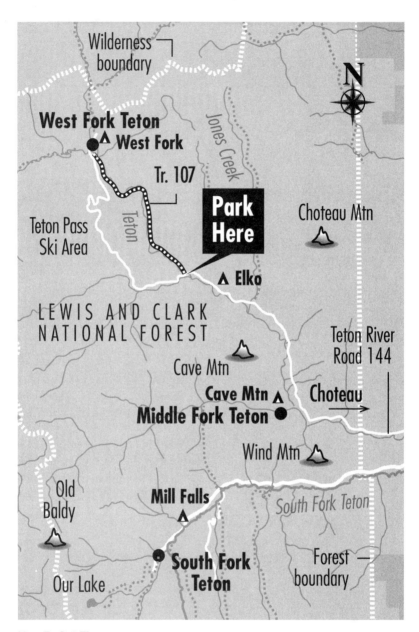

How To Get There

Proceed north out of Choteau on U.S. 89 to the Teton River Road 27 miles to just below where Waldron Creek spills into the Teton River. There's a good sign announcing Trail No. 107, the North Fork Trail. If you're taking two cars, park the second near an outhouse by an obvious horse saddling area not far from the West Fork cabin bridge.

ⓘ 22 North Fork Teton River Canyon

 Distance
Point-to-point walk-through is about 4 miles. Roundtrip is 8 miles.

 Difficulty
Moderate because of stream crossings. 3 on a scale of 5, with 5 being the hardest.

 Time Needed
4-5 hours for the walk-through.

Best Time
In the heat of summer, but good from early summer to late fall.

What You'll See
Limestone canyon cliffs that tower above the trail. Cold, clear, emerald green water.

 Cautions
If you do the hike from the Teton Canyon Road to the West Fork, you're going to get wet because of multiple stream crossings.

Sidetrips
The West Fork ending point is the hub for numerous trails.

 Camping
Elko with 3 campsites. Cave Mountain, 14 campsites. West Fork, 6 campsites.

Maps
Lewis and Clark National Forest Visitors Map, Rocky Mountain Division, (1988), Bob Marshall, Great Bear and Scapegoat Wilderness Complex Map, USGS Mount Wright topo.

Contacts
Rocky Mountain Ranger District, Choteau, (406) 466-5341; Lewis and Clark National Forest Supervisor's Office, Great Falls, 791-7700.

Hikers on the North Fork of the Teton River canyon.

Hesitating before walking into one of the cold, clear crossings.

Mount Wright looms above the trail.

You won't find better mountain views in the Rocky Mountain Front than those you'll find on Mount Wright (elevation 8,875 feet).

It's what makes spending the energy to cover the 8-mile trek worthwhile.

What's nice is that it is on trail all the way.

On top are breathtaking views of the limestone upthrusts of the Front exemplified by Choteau Mountain. Your Mount Wright perch is so good that you can peer over the top of the Front to see the "island" mountain ranges of central Montana, like the Sweetgrass Hills, the Bearpaws, Highwoods, and Belts. To the west you get views across the Bob Marshall showing off peaks like Pentagon and Silvertip and Swan and Holland summits on the Swan Range. To the north, Glacier National Park's summits are visible and recognizable, like the

finger of Mount St. Nicholas.

The Mount Wright Trail No. 160, constructed by Youth Conservation Corps, quickly leaves the clearcut and plunges into the forest, gradually picking up elevation.

It weaves its way up the southeast flank of the mountain, skirting a limestone ridge that runs down most of its length and depositing the hiker on an open area about 1,000 feet below the summit.

Here the trail switchbacks across an open face to the ridgeline. In mid-June to early July after the snowfields have cleared, the ground is resplendent with wildflowers.

On a cloudless and not so windy day, this can be a most glorious walk to the top. We've hiked and skied this mountain when the wind has been hurricane-force, not uncommon in these parts.

On top are the broken shards of glass and debris of a former Forest Service lookout. A cube-shaped building was put there in 2002 by the Forest Service to improve emergency radio communications in the back-country.

Pause here for a long break to drink in the beauty around you before heading back down.

Coming off Mount Wright with twilight illuminating the Front.

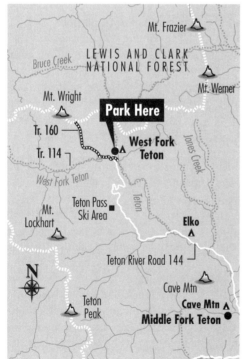

How To Get There

From Choteau go 5 miles north on U.S. 89 to the Teton River Road that is marked with good signs. The road is paved some 18 miles to the national forest boundary and is good gravel from there. Follow past the Teton Pass Ski Area on a good road that heads straight down into the Teton River bottom, losing 600 feet over about 4 miles. The trailhead is for the West Fork Trail No. 114, which is gated, about 33 miles from where you started on the Teton Road. Park here. The trail follows an old logging road past a clearcut for about a half mile where it intersects with the Mount Wright Trailhead No. 160.

23 Mount Wright

 Distance
Round trip of about 8 miles.

 Difficulty
Strenuous. A 4 on a scale of 5, with 5 being most difficult because of a 3,200+ feet of elevation gain.

Time Needed
6-8 hours.

Best Time
Late May until snow closes the road beyond the ski area in November.

What You'll See
Some of the best views on the Rocky Mountain Front. To the west, clear across the Bob Marshall Wilderness Area to the Swan Range. To the north, into Glacier Park Mount St. Nicholas is visible. To the south, the high Teton peaks, like Baldy and Rocky and Ear Mountain. To the east, the back side of the Front, particularly massive Choteau Mountain.

Cautions
Grizzly country. High winds.

 Sidetrips
Mount Wright sits above the North and West forks of the Teton River, the center of a hub of trails. The West Fork Trail leads to Teton Pass on the Continental Divide. The North Fork Trail No. 107 can be picked up at the West Fork administrative cabin and takes the hiker into the Bob Marshall Wilderness in a mile.

 Camping
West Fork Campground, 6 campsites.

 Maps
Lewis and Clark National Forest Visitors Map, Rocky Mountain Division, (1988), Bob Marshall, Great Bear and Scapegoat Wilderness Complex Map, USGS Mount Wright topo.

Contacts
Rocky Mountain Ranger District, Choteau, (406) 466-5341; Lewis and Clark National Forest Supervisor's Office, Great Falls, 791-7700.

The views from the top of Mount Wright are among the best in the Front.

A late spring view from the top of Mount Wright looking into the Bob Marshall Wilderness.

A long ridge walk to Washboard Reef awaits climbers from Teton Pass.

The Teton Pass hike travels land that has been freshly minted part of the Bob Marshall Wilderness in the Rocky Mountain Front Heritage Act: the West Fork Addition to the Bob.

This 10.8-mile round trip is also a quick route from the east side of the Continental Divide to the west side and the Flathead National Forest.

Begin the hike at the West Fork Teton Trailhead for Trail No. 114, the same trail you would take to begin the hike to the top of Mount Wright.

In less than a mile, that Mount Wright trail No. 160 enters from the right.

Continue straight ahead.

Most of this hike is in forest that occasionally breaks out in grass meadows or scree slopes, providing good views of the Continental Divide.

In roughly two miles, the Olney Creek Trail No. 117 (that wraps around

the back side of Mount Lockhart) comes in from the left along a creek bottom.

At this point you are in the Wright Creek drainage, a huge hunk of wild land flanked by the west slope of Mount Wright and an extension of the Corrugate Ridge. There are pretty good elk trails through heavy timber that will take you into this roadless track if you are inclined to leave the trail to explore.

The trail stays above the West Fork almost all the way to its source at Teton Pass, where there are Bob Marshall Flathead National Forest signs.

If you are looking for a great off-trail ridge walk side-trip, head south along the divide that leads to Washboard Reef. The divide rises and falls, climbing nice, unnamed peaks along the way. I've then dropped down the Olney Creek trail and out to complete a 15-mile loop. I highly recommend at least getting to the top of the ridge once you've attained Teton Pass. The views of the Bob, particularly the ridge line and Wrong Creek are very impressive.

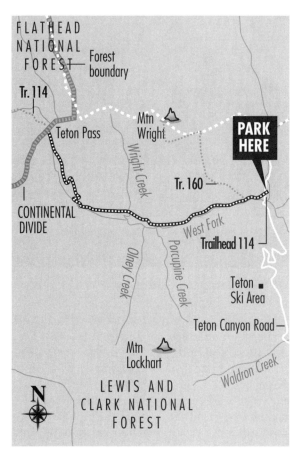

How To Get There

From Choteau go 7 miles north on U.S. 89 to the Teton County (Canyon) Road that is marked with good signs. The road is paved some 18 miles to the national forest boundary and is good gravel from there. Follow past the Teton Pass Ski Area. Drive past the ski area on a good road that heads straight down into the Teton River bottom, losing 600 feet over about four miles. The trailhead is for the West Fork Trail No. 114, which is gated, about 33 miles from where you started on the Teton Road. Park here. The trail follows an old logging road past a clearcut for about a half mile where it intersects with the Mount Wright Trailhead No. 160. Continue straight ahead.

24 Teton Pass

Distance
Round trip of about 10.8 miles and elevation gain of 2,008 feet.

Difficulty
Difficult. A 4 on a scale of 5, with 5 being most difficult because of the distance

Time Needed
6-8 hours.

Best Time
June until snow closes the road beyond the ski area in November.

What You'll See
Wild country in deep forest in a new wilderness area addition to the Bob Marshall. Near the pass there are open slopes and great views of the Continental Divide ridge line.

Cautions
Grizzlies. High winds.

Sidetrips
Climb Mount Wright; explore Olney Creek; continue on to the Washboard Reef along the Continental Divide ridge line.

Camping
West Fork Campground, 6 campsites.

Maps
Lewis and Clark National Forest Visitors Map, Rocky Mountain Division, (1988), Bob Marshall, Great Bear and Scapegoat Wilderness Complex Map, USGS Mount Wright topo.

Contacts
Rocky Mountain Ranger District, Choteau, (406) 466-5341; Lewis and Clark National Forest Supervisor's Office, Great Falls, 791-7700.

Approaching Teton Pass.

The wilderness sign buried in snow at Teton Pass.
(Mark Hertenstein photo)

Mount Werner pokes its head up above the Muddy Creek Falls canyon.

Over the years I've cheated myself out of some spectacular sights on the Rocky Mountain Front in pursuit of its tallest peaks.

I made an exception for the Muddy Creek Falls and am glad I did.

It is one of the most accessible and yet more visually pleasing sights on the Front and is a "must see" for those with limited time or energy. The falls are a spectacular counterpoint to the otherwise dry Front. It reminded me of falls in Zion National Park.

You'll hear the falls before you get there. You'll snake through a canyon before reaching them.

After leaving the parking area, go to the road bottom and follow it, where you'll come to a capped gas well in about a mile. This is where the road ends. Look ahead and locate the slot canyon and head for it, crossing back and forth across the shallow creek.

You'll be looking at Mount Werner (elevation 8,090 feet) to the west and a little north.

It is about a mile from the well to the slot canyon.

The insides of the slot are cave-like, cool and shaded, a welcome break on a hot day in this otherwise unshaded territory.

Given the volume of water coming over the falls, you'll find it surprising how little water there is in the creek. When I visited one September, the creek was dry until I got within a half mile of the slot canyon. Then there was plenty of water.

I was delighted by the giant rock wedged over the top of the slot just above the falls.

The slot is a great place for a lunch and tough to leave.

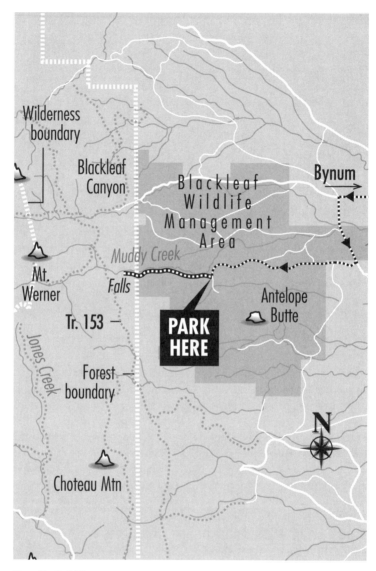

How To Get There

Out of Bynum, travel up the Blackleaf Road 13.9 miles to the Blackleaf Wildlife Management Area road juncture. Turn left (west) and drive one mile to the Blackleaf sign (you'll know it by the white arrows). Turn left (south) and proceed 1.4 miles. Turn right and go .5 miles and turn right onto a two track road. Another .2 miles and you'll reach an arched gate. Travel 2.5 miles on this road to an obvious parking area where there's a locked gate. Get out, go around the gate and within about 100 feet take the fork to the right and walk 2 miles to the falls along the creek bottom.

25 Muddy Creek Falls

 Distance
About 4 miles round trip.

 Difficulty
Easy to moderate. 2 on a scale of 5, with 5 the hardest. Route-finding. Little elevation gain. No path.

 Time Needed
2-3 hours.

 Best Time
Early summer until winter, when the Blackleaf Game Management Area is closed from Dec. 1 to May 15.

 What You'll See
A 50-foot waterfall at the end of a slot canyon reminiscent of what you'd see in Zion or Bryce Canyon national parks in Utah.

 Cautions
Grizzly country. Rocky bottom.No official trail.

 Sidetrips
Nearby Blackleaf Canyon

 Camping
Camping is possible at the trailhead. There are several undesignated and undeveloped areas just east of the trailhead in the Blackleaf Wildlife Management Area.

 Maps
U.S. Forest Service Bob Marshall, Great Bear, Scapegoat Wilderness Complex, 2011. Lewis and Clark National Forest Rocky Mountain Division Visitors Map. USGS Volcano Reef topo.

 Contacts
Lewis and Clark National Forest in Great Falls, 791-7700, Rocky Mountain Ranger District, Choteau, (406) 466 5341.

Muddy Creek Falls in a tight canyon.

Views above the Blindhorse Canyon.

The U.S. Bureau of Land Management has four Outstanding Natural Areas along the Rocky Mountain Front and all are difficult to access.

The Blindhorse Outstanding Natural Area is one of these.

It is an exceptionally beautiful area perched on a grass bench beneath several unnamed mountains to the north of Choteau Mountain. A lovely, narrow limestone canyon works its way up the North Fork of Blindhorse Creek. Most of the year the creek is free of water and is a good way to work your way down to your car.

Because of the access difficulty, I'll spend a little time giving you some options.

Option 1:

This option allows you to access the area without getting landowner permission.

It is a bit complicated and involves cross-country travel.

Dan Bennett of Great Falls described it this way to me, and I have taken this up-and-back route:

"Follow the country road described below to the southern boundary of the Blackleaf Wildlife Management Area. The boundary is marked by a sign. There is a cattle guard just north of you. Next, climb over the gate into the Blackleaf and walk a mile to a mile and a half west along the fence line. Eventually you hit a fence running north-south marking the boundary between the Blackleaf and BLM land.

"Hop the fence and head south of the mouth of Blindhorse Creek (quarter mile). Walk the canyon to where the creek forks (about a mile). Take the left fork south and there will be a trail that takes you along the south fork. It brings you quickly out of the creekbed on the right (west) side.

"Once out, head generally west and you will find the rough natural gas exploration road. Follow the road about 1.75 miles onto the Blindhorse Outstanding Natural Area where it hooks up with the Pamburn Creek Trail No. 153.

"Follow that north a half mile to find the North Fork of Blindhorse Creek, which you'll use to get back. About midway down the canyon there's an old shack on the north bank. Follow the canyon back 2 miles to the forks at the west end of the main canyon.

"From there it is just a matter of retracing your steps. With any luck the sunset will be behind you as you recross the flats," said Bennett.

Option 2:

Gene Sentz of Choteau says he's been to the Blindhorse "every way possible." He swears by the 1962 road through George Widener's property. Widener lives in Columbia Falls, although he has a house in Choteau. Contact Widener

How To Get There

From Choteau U.S. 89 7 miles north to the Teton River Road. Take the road 13 miles and look for a good gravel cutoff road marked Blackleaf Canyon that angles northwest toward the Canyon. It's about another 7 miles to the trailhead. About a half-mile past a little lake in Section 10, T25N, R8W, the road makes a big switchback across the Clark Fork of Muddy Creek. If you have landowner permission, park near the old shed, walk west up an old road and go through the locked gate.

Once here, another way to begin this route is to drive to the southern boundary of the Blackleaf Wildlife Management Area (about three-quarters of a mile beyond the start point above) and work your way along the fence lines until getting onto public land. Your goal is a well-worn seismic road that takes you directly into the Blindhorse Outstanding Area.

It is also possible, but much longer, to walk in from Clary Coulee or Blackleaf Canyon along Trail No. 177, which would be 10 strenuous miles roundtrip.

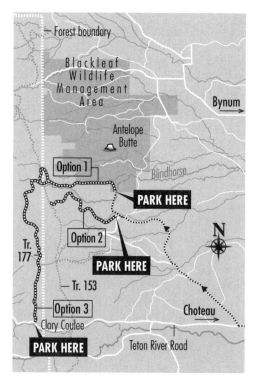

26 Blindhorse

 Distance
If you come up from the bottom, 6-7 miles roundtrip. If you use Clary Coulee or Blackleaf Canyon routes, 10-12 miles.

 Difficulty
Moderately strenuous, a 4 on a scale of 5, with 5 the hardest, because the destination may be hard to find and there is some off trail and unmarked road to follow.

 Time Needed
6-8 hours.

Best Time
Late spring to late fall.

 What You'll See
This is the "heart" of the Front and has a little bit of everything. You're in transition territory, where the land goes from prairie, travels through a deep limestone canyon, comes out onto grasslands and climaxes at the foot of towering Front peaks. What makes this area particularly interesting is that it has been at the center of a controversy over oil and gas development.

 Cautions
Grazing permitted.

 Sidetrips
In the Blindhorse Area, check out the scenery along Trail No. 177 that travels along the base of the Front. The unnamed mountain at the head of Blindhorse is climbable from the west side.

 Camping
If you start at Clary Coulee, there's nearby Cave Mountain Campground at the mouth of the Middle Fork of Teton River. The Blindhorse is prime backpacking country.

 Maps
Lewis and Clark National Forest Map (Rocky Mountain Division); Bob Marshall, Great Bear, and Scapegoat Wilderness Complex Map, BLM Choteau Mountain map, USGS Volcano Reef and Cave Mountain topo maps.

Contacts
Lewis and Clark National Forest in Great Falls, 791-7700, Rocky Mountain Ranger District, Choteau, (406) 466 5341. BLM office in Great Falls, 791-7700, Lewistown office, (406) 538-7461.

or the Montana Wilderness Association to get access.

Here's Sentz's description:

"Go through the locked gate and on to the top of the little bench in the northeast quarter of Section 9. There's a stone there with 'Old North Trail' engraved on it. The dirt road goes south down over to the Surfening Ranch. Don't go that way. Cut a sharp right to the northwest and stay on the seismic road. It takes you around and through another gate by a spring box (from there the map shows the two-track as a dotted line trail) and on up the draw into an open flat where an old 1960s drill site was (the only way you can distinguish it is by the different vegetation and weeds).

"A little way beyond that you move into the timber on BLM land and the road gets much steeper as you parallel the main fork of Blindhorse Creek. It's about 2 more miles up the main bench, and there's a wire gate up there just before you drop over to a little pond in Section 6."

Option 3:
Follow Trail No. 177 out of Clary Coulee or Blackleaf Canyon on Trail No.

153 heading south, or Trail No. 153 heading north up Pamburn Creek. If you choose the Clary Coulee route, you'll eventually encounter an error in the maps which shows a link between Trails 177 and 153. That link doesn't exist and you'll do some route-finding to get into the Blindhorse. It will mean dropping down a dry waterfall bed at the head of Blindhorse. This is a scramble for experienced hikers and a bit tricky, but doable.

Here's Sentz's preferred route that links the two trails:

"On your map, find Section 18, T25N, R8W, and you'll see where the Chicken Coulee trail comes up from the east to hook into 153. If you keep poking around pretty much due west up that draw (just on the north side), you'll eventually find an old trail. We ride it horseback. It's about 3 miles south of where the nonexistent trail is shown on the USFS map.

"If you're coming up Pamburn Creek on 153 from the south, as soon as you go through the gate at the very head of Pamburn and start dropping north down into Chicken Coulee, bear to the west and cross the draw (to the north side) and you'll find that old trail."

Passing through the Blackleaf Canyon.

You don't have to go very far to get the full effect of a hike through the Blackleaf Canyon.

A good gravel road brings you to Trail No. 106 and the gates of this canyon, whose limestone walls thrust directly up.

Don't be surprised to see rope climbers hanging like spiders off these breathtaking walls. It has become an increasingly popular place for climbers to enjoy their extreme sport. Routes have been developed and mapped.

It is ironic that the pedestrian hiker can enjoy an easy walk down below where Blackleaf Creek has cut its path.

Pack a picnic lunch and walk through the canyon which opens up into an amphitheater below Werner and Frazier peaks with seating on grass filled with tons of wildflowers.

You can walk a mile or less and you'll have had one of the scenic feasts of the Rocky Mountain Front.

For the more adventuresome, there's plenty else to do here.

I've used Blackleaf Canyon as a jumping-off point for the ambitious walk across the Front to Clary Coulee via the Blindhorse Canyon along cut-across Trail No. 153. One of the best-kept secrets of the Front is the splendor of the 8-mile hike from Blackleaf Canyon back to the West Fork of the Teton River via the East Fork that carries you into the Bob Marshall Wilderness Area.

Mount Werner is an easy scramble from the divide between the Blackleaf and Teton drainages.

Blackleaf is also a great place to begin off-trail climbs of Frazier or Old Man of the Hills mountain peaks. There is also an ambitious and partly off-trail hike around Volcano Reef that starts here, too: 153/106, the off trail coming in the South Fork of Dupuyer Creek.

Exploration and development for oil and gas here have been at the heart of the battle for the Rocky Mountain Front, with environmentalists pointing to it as a precursor of what happened in Alberta's Front, and developers pointing to it as proof that the resource is present.

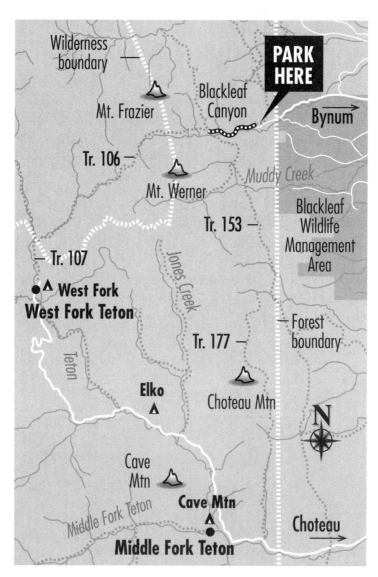

How To Get There

About 85 miles northwest of Great Falls. Drive to Bynum. Take a good gravel county road some 15 miles west of Bynum to the canyon.

27 Blackleaf Canyon

 Distance
It is about a mile from the parking lot through the canyon to a broad, open valley. It is 6.5 miles, about 4-6 hours round-trip if the Blackleaf-East Fork Divide is chosen.

Difficulty
Easy. 1 on a scale of 5, with 1 being easiest. A 3 if the hike is to the Blackleaf/East Fork Teton Divide

 Time Needed
As much as you need, or 4-6 hours if hiking to the divide.

Best Time
Late spring through early winter.

 What You'll See
Spectacular tight canyon with limestone walls that rise several hundred feet above the valley floor.

Cautions
Grizzly habitat, wind.

Sidetrips
Both Mounts Werner and Frazier can be climbed via the Blackleaf Canyon. There is a nice 8-mile point-to-point hike to the East Fork of the Teton via Trails No. 106/107. For the rope climber, numerous routes have been developed on these walls.

 Camping
Camping is possible at the trailhead. There are several undesignated and undeveloped areas just east of the trailhead in the Blackleaf Wildlife Management Area.

Maps
U.S. Forest Service Bob Marshall, Great Bear, Scapegoat Wilderness Complex, 2011. Lewis and Clark National Forest Rocky Mountain Division Visitors Map. USGS Volcano Reef topo.

 Contacts
Lewis and Clark National Forest in Great Falls, 791-7700, Rocky Mountain Ranger District, Choteau, (406) 466-5341.

The Blackleaf wall is attractive to technical climbers.

28 North Fork Dupuyer Canyon

Looking through the canyon on the North Fork of Dupuyer Creek.

The trip to the Dupuyer Creek trailhead No. 124 is an adventure in itself, but is well worth the effort because it delivers you to a spectacular canyon, and hiking opportunities that could involve a climb of Old Man of the Hills or Bennie Hill.

The North Fork Dupuyer Canyon is very similar to the Blackleaf Canyon, but grander. The walls are higher and smoother, the creek faster and with more water in it than Blackleaf Creek, and the area much more pristine since Blackleaf has been logged, roaded and subjected to natural gas development, and is easier to get to.

You pass between Old Man of the Hills and Walling Reef mountains. This would be a much better way to climb Walling Reef than the much more accessible Swift Dam trailhead via Phillips Creek traverse that I had done some years ago. The trail up the North Fork

climbs to a high pass below a massive, unnamed ridge to the west and south. There are side trails up Canyon Creek that parallels Walling Reef and Potshot Creek that sits below Bennie Hill.

To get up Bennie Hill (elevation 7,830 feet) take the Potshot trail, and attain the southeast ridge of the mountain. It is about 2,500 feet to the top, which is reminiscent of Beartop lookout in the Bob Marshall above the North Fork of the Sun River. There are steep limestone outcrops along the ridgeline.

There are remains of an old wilderness fire lookout at the top of the mountain.

There are wonderful views of Patrick Gass, Bumshot, Drewyer, Crooked, Fields and Sentinel mountains to the west, and spectacular views of the Rocky Mountain Front peaks to the east.

Bennie Hill was named for a small

boy who had accompanied a forest ranger on a horseback ride in this area. It was hard to imagine how supplies were hauled to this steep mountain; I suspect from the pass above the North Fork and then up a ridgeline to the top of Bennie Hill.

If you're up for an exploration of an off-trail route up Old Man of the Hills Mountain, once through the canyon head up the first drainage to the south (Washout Creek), and a route becomes obvious along a ridgeline immediately to the west. There will be a short knife ridge to the summit cap, but nothing serious.

This is bear country, so keep your eyes open!

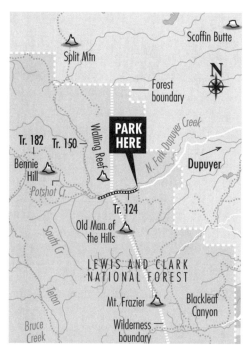

How To Get There

The best way to describe the route to the trailhead is to go to Dupuyer, find the Dupuyer Creek Road in town. Travel west on this excellent gravel road 8 miles to the TR Memorial Ranch road. Head south on this road taking the left fork at the Boone and Crockett Theodore Roosevelt Memorial Ranch. It is about 2.5 miles of good gravel between the Dupuyer Road and next main thoroughfare road where you'll see the "Watchable Wildlife" sign. Turn left here. Travel west another two miles of again, good gravel, and the road forks again. Take the right fork that drops right into a creek bottom and your first stream crossing. This is where the road gets really rough all the way to the trailhead, some four miles west and three more stream crossings and several gates. There's a good parking area about 2 miles from the first stream crossing. If you value your car you'll park here and walk in. If you drive all the way you'll need a high clearance vehicle and four wheel.

28 North Fork Dupuyer Canyon

 Distance
As far as you'd like to go. It is less than a mile through the canyon.

Difficulty
Easy. The walk through the canyon, less than a mile, is an easy trek.

 Time Needed
Less than an hour unless you decide to climb one of the alluring peaks back in this country.

 Best Time
Summer, to avoid getting mired in one of the road's mudholes.

 What You'll See
A spectacular limestone canyon that rises abruptly from the valley floor. It is a short walk into this Bob Marshall Wilderness Area wonderland.

Cautions
Terrible access road.

Sidetrips
This is the shortest way to climb Walling Reef, accessed by taking the Canyon Creek Trail No. 150, and scrambling up the back side. It is also a quick way to climb Old Man of the Hills Peak via Washout Creek

 Maps
U.S. Forest Service Bob Marshall, Great Bear, Scapegoat Wilderness

Contacts
Lewis and Clark National Forest in Great Falls, 791-7700, Rocky Mountain Ranger District, Choteau, (406) 466-5341.

Climbers gut it out on Old Man of the Hills mountain.

Walling Reef is a dominant mountain on the north flank of the canyon.

Swift Dam on Birch Creek offers several trailheads.

Like Gibson Reservoir on the Sun River, the other great water impoundment on the Rocky Mountain Front, Swift Reservoir on Birch Creek, is a hub for trails and a major jumping-off point for Bob Marshall Wilderness Area trips.

Only this is a bit more remote and takes some effort getting to, although the access road is great.

It takes a drive to Dupuyer, 90 miles from Great Falls off U.S. 89, and then another 18 miles to Swift Dam.

For beauty, the drive itself is worth the trip. I've seen grizzlies and a good-sized elk herd on the flat to the east within a mile of the campsite. Vast aspen groves on the hillsides light up in the fall.

This is where the mountains of the Front are included in the Bob Marshall.

The good gravel road takes a direct shot to a wall of mountains dominated by Walling Reef (elevation 7,925 feet) on the south. To the north, the mountains of the Badger-Two Medicine Wilderness Study Area, with Heart Butte (elevation 6,863 feet) acting like a sentinel on the Great Plains above the Blackfeet Indian Reservation. Mount Richmond (elevation 8,177 feet) towers over Swift Reservoir and is within the Bob Marshall.

Swift Dam hovers above a washed-out Birch Creek valley floor that still holds evidence of the 1964 flood that destroyed the dam, resulting in human death and property damage.

There is limited access to the reservoir from both sides.

To the south, it is on the trail above the BLM campsite.

To the north, by road across the Blackfeet reservation where a $10 annual permit is required. It is an additional charge for a Blackfeet fishing permit. Great Falls and businesses in the the small Rocky Mountain Front communities like Dupuyer, Bynum, Valier, Browning and Choteau carry them.

The north road is the quickest way into the Badger-Two Medicine Wilderness Study Area, but the south Trail No. 143 hooks up with cut-across Trail No. 105 that travels around the north end of the reservoir and hooks up with Trail No. 121, the North Fork of Birch Creek Trail.

A good introductory 10-mile roundtrip hike is to that point.

What you'll see is great peaks of the Front and Bob, the shores of aqua-colored Swift Reservoir, and Birch Creek in a canyon.

There are obvious spots to access the reservoir shore.

At 1.3 miles look for Hellroaring Spring, a great place to refill your water bottle or pack.

The Phillips Creek Trail No. 150, at the 2-mile mark, is a way to access Walling Reef.

A short distance later you'll have to use some rocks to get across Phillips Creek.

At 3 miles there's another ford, this time across Birch Creek, where the water can be ice cold and thigh deep. I generally bring water sandals with me to make this crossing.

This is a logical turnaround point after lunch.

However, the scenery gets progressively more beautiful up the trail, particularly if you hike toward the Middle Fork of Birch Creek on Trail No. 123 another 1.5 miles.

Along this stretch the mountains line up on both sides of the trail.

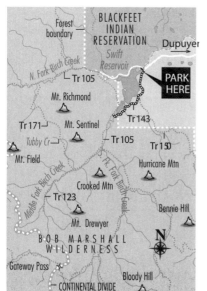

How To Get There

Access a good gravel road just north of Dupuyer adjacent to a state rest area, traveling west to the trailhead some 18 miles. There are trailheads on the north and south sides of the reservoir. The suggested hike is Trailhead No. 143 accessed south of the dam near a BLM campsite.

29 Swift Dam

 Distance
If you go to the junction of Trail No. 105, the cut across to the North Fork of Birch Creek, about 10 miles roundtrip.

Difficulty
Moderate. About a 3 on a scale of 5, with 5 being most difficult, because of some elevation gain and loss.

 Time Needed
4-6 hours.

Best Time
Late spring through early winter.

 What You'll See
This is where the mountains of the Front are included in the Bob Marshall Wilderness Area, and the waters flowing from these mountains, the forks of Birch Creek, are impounded behind Swift Dam in a reservoir where the water is an aqua-blue color. Along the way you'll encounter a large spring (Hellroaring), fishing access, alpine scenery and stream crossings.

 Cautions
Adjacent lands are on the Blackfeet Reservation, and a tribal permit is required,

which can be purchased in nearby communities and Great Falls.

Sidetrips
This is a major access point into the north end of the Bob Marshall Wilderness Area. Climbable mountains line up on both sides of the trail, Hurricane Ridge, Drewyer, Sentinel, to name a few. This is also a great backpacking area, particularly up the Middle Fork of Birch Creek.

 Camping
There is a BLM campsite at the end of the road on the south side of the dam.

Maps
U.S. Forest Service Bob Marshall, Great Bear, Scapegoat Wilderness Complex, 2011. Lewis and Clark National Forest Rocky Mountain Division Visitors Map. USGS Swift Reservoir, and Gateway Pass topos.

Contacts
Lewis and Clark National Forest in Great Falls, 791-7700, Rocky Mountain Ranger District, Choteau, (406) 466-5341.

Coming off Mount Drewyer in Swift Dam country with Mount Field in the background.

The North Fork of Birch Creek runs a steely blue color.

Curious about the Badger-Two Medicine Wilderness Study Area but are baffled about how to access it easily?

The North Fork of Birch Creek Trail No. 121 provides an easy gateway to this area marked by mythological Blackfeet names like Poia, Scarface, Feather Woman and Morningstar mountains, all prominent characters in that tribe's Sun Dance story.

It is also a superhighway into the Bob Marshall Wilderness Area where there are several good loop hikes that shoot off the trail.

It is heavily forested here, with most of the daylight provided by the valley floor of steely blue North Fork of Birch Creek.

I suggest a 3.5-mile walk up the North Fork to the spot where Blind-Tubby Creek Trail No. 171 comes in from the south. Along the way, spend some time at Killem Horse Creek to view a waterfall and explore a trail-less canyon.

Aside from a couple of hundred feet uphill from where you park at the mouth of Haywood Creek, there is very little elevation gain and loss along this trail until it rises to the pass below Family Peak, some 5 miles up the trail.

The beauty of this trail is the access it gives you to other trails.

You find this trailhead by traveling around the north side of Swift Reservoir. The road is rough and bumpy and even narrow during its 1.5 miles to Haywood Creek.

There is an obvious place for parking before the road plunges across Haywood Creek.

Then it is a walk uphill where the road quickly meets Trail No. 105 that continues south around the west end of Swift Reservoir on its way to the South

Fork of Birch Creek

Instead, bear to your right (or west), and you're on Trail No. 121 that travels the floor of the North Fork, dropping at times across the creek.

This fork is an icy blue-gray color and shoots through a narrow canyon at points and drops over several sets of waterfalls. I like the falls where Killem Horse Creek empties into the North Fork. There's a nice backpack camp just beyond the falls.

About 2 miles from your car you'll come to Trail No. 122 that lies in a broad wash of Man Creek and heads north into the Badger-Two Medicine Wilderness Study Area behind a mountain named Major Steele Backbone before heading to the pass between Feather Woman Mountain and Heart Butte.

Killem Horse is less than a mile west of this trail junction and runs up a spectacular trail-less canyon to the foot of Mount Poia. It is worthwhile to spend some time exploring this canyon and enjoying the falls.

I've used the ridgeline to the north between Killem Horse and Blind Creek junction to climb Poia.

In less than a mile the Blind Creek-Tubby Creek Trail No. 171 comes in from the south. This trail runs between Mounts Field and Richmond before joining the Middle Fork trail at the base of Mount Sentinel.

You can turn around here and return the 3.5 miles back to your car.

If you continue ahead, the trail rises slightly and passes through a scree slope before dropping back down to the bot-

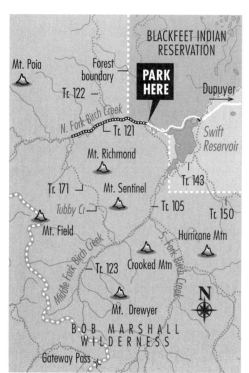

How To Get There

Access a good gravel road just north of Dupuyer adjacent to a state rest area, traveling west to the trailhead, some 18 miles. There are trailheads on the north and south sides of the reservoir. The suggested hike is Trailhead No. 121, north of the dam. Before you reach the spillway, cross Birch Creek and proceed 1.5 miles along a rough one-track road along the north side of the dam to a parking area just before you get to Haywood Creek. Park here, cross the creek and proceed uphill to a trail junction of Trails No. 121 and No. 105. Continue west along No. 121.

ℹ 30 North Fork of Birch Creek

Distance
If you go to the junction of Trail No. 171 (Tubby Creek), the cut across to the Middle Fork of Birch Creek, about 7 miles round trip.

Difficulty
Moderate. About a 3 on a scale of 5, with 5 being most difficult, because of some elevation gain and loss and stream crossings.

Time Needed
4-6 hours.

Best Time
Late spring through early winter.

What You'll See
This is a hike in a forested valley that is flanked by massive Mount Richmond on the south. There are numerous small waterfalls and water chutes on this trail.

Cautions
Adjacent lands are on the Blackfeet Reservation, and a tribal permit is required. Permits can be purchased in nearby communities and Great Falls.

Sidetrips
This is a major access point into the north end of the Bob Marshall Wilderness Area. This is a good access to off-trail climbing of Family, Scarface and Poia mountains in the Badger-Two Medicine Wilderness Study Area. This is also a great backpacking area with good campsites at the various creeks that intersect the trail: Steep, Small, Killem Horse and Hungry Man creeks. For the ambitious, a good 15-mile loop hike traverses around Mount Richmond by way of Tubby Creek to the Middle Fork of Birch Creek.

Camping
There is a BLM campsite at the end of the road on the south side of the dam.

Maps
U.S. Forest Service Bob Marshall, Great Bear, Scapegoat Wilderness Complex, 2011. Lewis and Clark National Forest Rocky Mountain Division Visitors Map. USGS Swift Reservoir topo.

Contact
Lewis and Clark National Forest in Great Falls, 791-7700, Rocky Mountain Ranger District, Choteau, (406) 466-5341.

tom, where in about three-quarters of a mile, Small Creek dumps in from the north. Here again, is an ideal backpack camp spot.

I've used the ridge on the west side of Small Creek to climb Scarface Mountain. It is possible to use the ridge on the east side to climb Poia.

From Small Creek it is another mile to Steep Creek, which drains Emerald Lake, in an alpine cirque on the northern flank of Family peak. It is a rough 2-mile bushwhack into this seldom-visited lake, which is clearly visible from the Scarface ridgeline.

The trail then begins a 1,400 foot, 2-mile rise to the pass below the southwest ridge of Family Peak and then on to Badger Pass.

The trail flanks Mount Richmond.

Looking down on Kiyo Crag Lake from the crag.

It takes some doing to get to the Palookaville trailhead in the Badger-Two Medicine Wilderness Study Area near Heart Butte.

It is as tough a trailhead as there is to find in the Lewis and Clark National Forest, but worth the effort.

The road sign number doesn't match the Forest Service Visitors map or the Bob Marshall Wilderness complex map's number. Both show the road number as 9218. The road sign shows 9128.

The road is a pretty rough drive, too. I wouldn't take my car in there in wet weather. The road is deeply rutted and rocky.

From Heart Butte, take the Heart Butte-Browning Road north about 8 miles to Little Badger Creek. Just north of the creek there's a road with a paved turnout coming in from the west. Take that about 1.5 miles where you'll see a

ranch house. There's a dirt track road with the brown Forest Service road sign No. 9128 on it. Follow that about 4.5 miles, where it intersects with a short road that drops to the trailhead. You'll find Forest Service Trail No. 172. The road you just left continues to the top of Mount Baldy! It is used to service the electronics equipment on the mountaintop. Some attain the Kiyo Crag ridgeline by driving to it rather than hiking to it as I did.

The trailhead is located in a place called "Palookaville." I thought it might be named for the mythical comics boxing character Joe Palooka. The Forest Service history card file doesn't give the derivation of the name. I've been told that Palookaville is a corruption of "Polackville," named for a rancher of Polish descent.

The trail itself is not well marked to

begin with. From the parking lot find a small path to your right and follow it across the creek and up a small rise. You're on the trail, although all the cattle trails make the going a bit confusing at times.

This is open country, and there aren't many trees that are capable of bearing the Forest Service trail-marking slashes.

It is an easy walk to the lake off a spur from the main Trail No. 172.

The walk to the lake is about 3 miles from the trailhead with the trail ascending some 800 feet to the lake over those miles.

This pleasant walk follows the North Fork of Little Badger Creek. Just beyond 2 miles there are a small waterfall and a bench. At this point start looking for the trails that fork to the west off the

main trail. These lead to Kiyo Crag Lake, a tarn scoured out by a glacier, that sits more than 1,000 feet below the Kiyo Crag ridgeline. The Montana Department of Fish, Wildlife and Parks stocks this lake with westslope cutthroat trout.

If you are more interested in climbing the peak and want to get to the ridgeline instead, you would go from the trailhead through open grass-filled slopes for about a mile and then get off, heading up toward some ledges that run parallel to, and above the creek. I walked these ledges, aiming for a saddle between Baldy Mountain and the Kiyo ridge. I eventually happened on the Baldy Road,

How To Get There

From Heart Butte take the Heart Butte-Browning Road north about 8 miles to Little Badger Creek. Just north of the creek there's a road with a paved turnout coming in from the west. Take that for about 1.5 miles where you'll see a ranch house. There's a dirt track road there with the brown Forest Service road sign No. 9128 on it. Follow that about 4.5 miles where it intersects with a short road that drops to the trailhead. You'll find Forest Service Trail No. 172. (The road you just left continues to the top of Mount Baldy! It is used to service the electronics equipment on the mountaintop.) Some attain the Kiyo Crag ridgeline by driving to it rather than hiking to it as I did. The trailhead is located in a place called "Palookaville."

31 Kiyo Crag Lake

 Distance
Just over 3 miles each way.

 Difficulty
Moderate. The most difficult part of this hike is trail-finding. Elevation gain is 800 feet. There is a small waterfall on the North Fork of Little Badger Creek. Start looking for trails angling toward the lake beyond the falls.

 Time Needed
The drive from Great Falls is the hard part, about 110 miles to the trailhead, some of it over tough road. I'd give myself 2 hours of hiking each way to the lake.

 Best Time
During dry summer and fall months, once the badly rutted road has dried.

What You'll See
Remote high mountain limestone ridges towering over aspen-grove-sprinkled grasslands. This country is grazed, so there may be cattle. There has been some four-wheeling as well. Because of the tough road it is seldom visited, except by those seeking out Kiyo Crag Lake. The lake is stocked with westslope cutthroat trout.

 Cautions
Grizzly country, rough roads.

 Sidetrips
Kiyo Crag ridge and peak above the lake is an easy scramble and broad ridge walk. As you walk up the trail, start looking for ways to gain the ridge. One other way to gain the ridge would be to walk or drive up the road to the top of Baldy and traverse over.

 Camping
You could set up camp at the trailhead.

 Maps
U.S. Forest Service Bob Marshall, Great Bear, Scapegoat Wilderness Complex, 2011. Lewis and Clark National Forest Rocky Mountain Division Visitors Map. BLM: Hungry Horse map; USGS Half Dome Crag topo.

Contacts
Lewis and Clark National Forest in Great Falls, 791-7700, Rocky Mountain Ranger District, Choteau, (406) 466-5341.

Kiyo Crag Mountain above Kiyo Crag Lake.

which took me to the saddle.

Then I had a magnificent stroll along the ridge at roughly 7,000 feet. I could see the alpine Kiyo Crag Lake below me 1,000 feet through limestone spires. Kiyo Crag, which means "bear mountain," is white limestone and has that classic Bob Marshall Wilderness look you'd find in the Augusta area mountains: reefs rising to peaks, punctuated by ledges. While the topo maps I looked at didn't indicate its height, my altimeter indicated it at just under 7,655 feet — about 2,300 feet of gain from the trailhead.

There is nothing hard about climbing this peak. It is a walkup with the last 200 feet limestone talus.

Views from the top include the southeast end of Glacier Park, the Bob Marshall and Great Bear wilderness areas to the west and the great plains over the Front to the east. I was able to pick out classic Glacier peaks like Rising Wolf, Summit and Divide as well as Great Northern and Grant peaks in the Great Bear. The heart of the Badger-Two Medicine Wilderness Study Area lay at my feet. The Blackfeet Reservation pothole lakes dotted the prairie.

On top you realize that it wouldn't be hard to continue on the ridgeline to the higher Half Dome Crag mountain. However, I suggest turning around and coming down the steep talus east ridgeline, connecting to a gentler north ridge and eventually gaining the trail.

*South Fork Two Medicine River below Elk Calf Mountain
in Badger-Two Medicine Area near Marias Pass.*

Marias Pass is the outer limit of the Front, on its northwest flank, about 150 miles from Great Falls. It sits in the shadows of Summit Mountain on the Continental Divide just 8 miles west of the town of East Glacier Park.

It is a great jumping off point for Glacier National Park across Highway 2 to the north or the Badger-Two Medicine Wilderness Study Area and Bob Marshall Wilderness Area to the south.

The Summit Campground is sheltered from the wind in the trees here, and there's even an historical obelisk marking this low point through the mountains at 5,236 feet, perfect for a highway and train traffic.

It is also perfect for getting quickly into the Front.

My recommendation is to set up camp at Summit and explore the Elk Calf Trail No. 137 for a distance. This is part of the Continental Divide Trail.

For the more ambitious, there's the Two Medicine-Elk Calf 19-mile loop, to which I will return.

The trail gains just over 2,800 feet to just below the top of Elk Calf (elevation 7,607 feet) and stays mostly in forest with occasional breaks that reveal the high country of the Two Medicine Ridge to the east and open park land. To the north there's the looming presence of Glacier Park. Like its neighbor to the north, this part of the Front is lush and richly vegetated.

The trail can be reached a number of ways.

At the Summit Campground, pick up the Trail No. 133 cut-across trail to the South Fork of the Two Medicine River. It climbs gradually out of the campground. You have to be patient if you want to enjoy this hike. You'll encounter four-wheeler ruts immediately. You pass a gas pipeline's right of way before entering the deep forest. It then starts to drop, and there are junctions to the south with the Elk Calf Trail No. 137 and horse packer-Trail No. 133.1, which comes up from below Marias Pass. Take Trail No. 137.

From Summit campground it is about 5.5 miles to the top of Elk Calf Mountain.

It is a pleasant walk north along the Continental Divide ridgeline about 2 miles north to Flattop Mountain, a favorite of backcountry snowshoers and skiers.

I began the Elk Calf-Two Medicine 19-mile loop at the Summit Campground the same way I suggested the Elk Calf trail jaunt and picked up the

Trail No. 133 cut-across trail that took me down to the South Fork of the Two Medicine River.

The trail drops through the forest to the South Fork, which was shallow enough to walk across without it going over my boots in late summer. This is where you pick up Trail No. 101 along the bottom of the South Fork. During spring's high water I could see the wade being challenging. Fall is definitely the time to do this hike when the water is low.

The walk is along an old road in a burn. The river passed through several rock canyons, and there were numerous little falls. Every time I turned north, I got views of Summit and Little Dog mountains in Glacier Park. To the west the Elk Calf ridge dominated.

How To Get There

Take Highway 2, 8 miles west of the town of East Glacier Park to Marias Pass. There's a large parking area there with adjacent trailheads.

32 Marias Pass

 Distance
Several miles for Elk Calf, 19 miles for Elk Calf-Two Medicine loop.

Difficulty
Moderate to More Difficult if taking a short up-and-back jaunt up Elk Calf Trail No. 137. Strenuous if taking the 19-mile Elk Calf-Two Medicine loop.

Time Needed
3 to 5 hours for a few miles on Elk Calf Trail; a 2-day backpack for the loop.

 Best Time
Early summer to early fall.

 What You'll See
Marias Pass is in the shadow of Summit and Little Dog mountains in Glacier National Park to the north. They dominate the scenery. There's an historic obelisk at the pass as well as the Summit campground in the Lewis and Clark National Forest. While Summit and Little Dog mountains rise precipitously to the north, the mountains on the Front to the south are low-slung and heavily forested and in some instances logged or reshaped by fire.

 Cautions
Grizzly country, changeable weather, obliterated trails, stream crossings, clearcuts.

 Sidetrips
Climb Elk Calf and Flattop mountains. Roundtrip to Elk Calf is 10.5 miles.

 Cross Country Skiing
Skiers use the area extensively going up the Elk Calf trail, climbing Flattop mountain and crossing Highway 2 to ski Autumn Creek in Glacier National Park.

 Maps
U.S. Forest Service Bob Marshall, Great Bear, Scapegoat Wilderness Complex, 2011. Lewis and Clark National Forest Rocky Mountain Division Visitors Map. BLM:

Hungry Horse map; USGS Summit topo.

 Contacts
Lewis and Clark National Forest in Great Falls, 791-7700, Rocky Mountain Ranger District, Choteau, (406) 466-5341.

I had originally set out to cut across to the Elk Calf Trail by way of a Trail No. 136 but couldn't find it below or on top although I looked hard for it. Having to take Trail No. 137 made my day longer, but it turned out to be worthwhile.

Although I enjoyed the river bottom, it was refreshing to finally reach a "real" trail when I got to No. 137. It narrowed down and was no longer rutted in any way. Four-wheelers are banned here.

Then it was an up-and-down stroll across the flanks of Elk Calf Mountain for the rest of the hike.

The trail has been beautifully reconstructed in recent years and is in great shape.

South Fork Two Med in Fall color.

While it is in deep forest most of the way, it is interesting because of the numerous creeks of which you drop in and out. Occasionally it opened up and offered tremendous views of the Two Medicine Ridge and river below.

As lovely as this trail is, I was concerned that someone had removed or altered trail signs at critical junctions. The most critical is a junction that leads to the top of Elk Calf Mountain. All signs were removed. Particularly because I couldn't find Trail No. 136, I had to really think through which way to go as

Trail No. 137 drops off sharply at this point. I followed it, hoping that I wasn't heading down No. 136 (I wasn't). Where the Pike Creek Trail No. 127 comes in, someone had carved a pointer in the sign going the wrong way (go west). I figured that out and went down this trail to cut some distance off the hike back to the campground.

This loop would make a nice backpack trip, especially along the river, where there are numerous good campsites. Trail No. 101 is also a direct shot into the Badger Cabin area.

Waterfalls of the Front

Although the Rocky Mountain Front is considered high and dry country, it abounds with waterfalls that drain its snowfields and empty its limestone caverns.

Some are those that you encounter on destination hikes such as the riffles and gushers along the banks of the Dearborn River through the Devil's Glen (See Hike No.2).

Nearby Falls Creek is aptly named, not only because of the large waterfall on private land adjacent to the Falls Creek Trailhead, but also because like the Dearborn, it drops over broken ledges and is spit through narrow chutes.

But there are a number of waterfalls mentioned in these pages that are destinations in themselves (See Willow Creek Falls Hike No. 9, Muddy Creek Falls Hike No.25).

There are two of note that are about a third of a mile from where you park your car: Cataract Falls off the Elk Creek Road near Augusta and Mill Falls off the South Fork of the Teton River.

There are also the unnamed waterfalls you see in the distance hiking to other destinations such as Route Creek Pass, Headquarters Pass, Crown Mountain and Our Lake.

The following are the "must see" waterfalls of the Front and how to get there:

The falls below Route Creek Pass.

Cataract Falls.

Cataract Falls

From Augusta, take Road 434 as if you are going to the Dearborn River. About 6 miles out of Augusta start looking for the Elk Creek Road. There's a road sign. Turn west onto this good, unpaved road and drive 17 miles to its end where you'll find Trail No. 205 and a good parking area. Cross Elk Creek, and the trail to the falls is marked with a sign. It is about a third of a mile to the falls, which can be heard crashing over ledges from the parking lot.

Mill Falls

The campground is located about a mile east of the parking lot for the Headquarters Pass/Our Lake trailhead. It is very small, with space for only 4 campsites. It is off the road, back in the trees and away from road noise — very secluded. At the end of the campground road is a sign pointing to the falls.

The falls are about 100 yards from this sign along an informal, flat trail. They spill about 30 feet over a cliff, which drains a small South-Fork-of-the-Teton feeder stream.

Willow Creek Falls

At Augusta, take the Benchmark Road some 15 miles to the Willow-Beaver Creek Road fork. Take the fork to the right and travel about a 1.5 miles to Camp Scoutana. Turn left onto the road. It is a fair two-track road to the trailhead, about 2 miles away. You know you're near when you come to a gate across the road. You can park there, or if you have enough clearance on your car, proceed to another barbed-wire gate where the trail begins. (See Hike No. 9)

Smith Creek Falls.

Muddy Creek Falls

Out of Bynum, travel up the Blackleaf Road 13.9 miles to the Blackleaf Wildlife Management Area road juncture. Turn left (west) and drive one mile to Blackleaf sign (you'll know it by the white arrows). Turn left (south) and proceed 1.4 miles. Turn right and go .5 miles and turn right onto a two-track road. Another .2 miles and you'll reach an arched gate. Travel 2.5 miles on this road to an obvious parking area where, there's a locked gate. Get out, go around the gate and within about 100 feet take the fork to the right and walk 2 miles to the falls along the creek bottom. (See Hike No. 25)

Smith Creek Falls

Park at the end of the Smith Creek Road about 3 miles south of Augusta on Road 434. Travel about 11 miles up the Smith Creek Road to Trail No. 215. Hike 2.1 miles through a working cattle ranch. It is a steep walk down into the falls from the trail, but well worth the effort.

Headquarters Pass Trail Falls

Take the Teton River Road 7 miles north of Choteau. It is the same road used to access the Teton Pass Ski Area. It is paved all of the way. At 18 miles, begin looking for a Forest Service sign indicating the road to the South Fork of the Teton Road 109, which you'll follow to its end, about 11 more miles. This parking lot serves the trail to both Headquarters Pass and Our Lake.

Park at the Our Lake/Headquarters Pass trailhead at the end of the South Fork of the Teton River Road, (See Hike No.16). There are two sets of falls, roughly a mile from the trailhead, one just before the switchbacks, another adjacent to the switchbacks.

Our Lake Trail Falls

Take the Teton River Road 7 miles north of Choteau. It is the same road used to access the Teton Pass Ski Area. It is paved much of the way. At 18 miles, begin looking for a Forest Service sign indicating the road to the South Fork of the Teton Road 109, which you'll follow to its end, about 11 more miles. This parking lot serves the trail to both Headquarters Pass and Our Lake.

Park at the Our Lake/Headquarters Pass trailhead at the end of the South Fork of the Teton River Road. There is a waterfall adjacent to the trail below the campsite. You can't miss it on the steep uphill just beyond the switchbacks. (See Hike No.17)

Dearborn River Falls

From Augusta, take State Highway No. 434 16 miles to the Bean Lake turnoff. Proceed about 8 miles to the end of the road where there's a gate across the road and the Trailhead No. 206 parking lot. The trail parallels the road for about a mile, where it crosses the Dearborn River bridge. You're still on private land here until you reach the Lewis and Clark National Forest sign, about another half-mile.

There are small waterfalls on the Dearborn River throughout The Devil's Glen hike.

Crown Mountain (Whitewater) Falls

At Augusta find the Forest Service Benchmark Road that will take you the 20 miles on good gravel to Crown Mountain Trailhead No. 270. About a mile up the trail you'll be able to see this falls through a clearing. It comes off the north face of the mountain and spills into Whitewater Creek.

Double Falls on Ford Creek

You'll find this dual cascade just off the road a little to the west of an undeveloped campground on Ford Creek on the Benchmark Road. Follow directions to get to the Crown Mountain falls (left). The campground is about a mile east of that trailhead. Park in the campground. It is a few hundred feet west.

Lange Falls

This falls is most reachable by water and drains out of Patricks Basin, about 3.5 miles up the south shore of Gibson Reservoir where Lange Creek empties into the lake. It is a short distance in from the cove.

Lange Falls at the head of Gibson Reservoir

Climbs

Among the great attractions of the Rocky Mountain Front are its stark, high, climbable mountains.

Most of the mountains rise between 1,500 feet to 3,000 feet above the valley floor.

The vast majority don't require technical mountain climbing skills or equipment.

They are straight line-of-sight scrambles. Most don't even require use of your hands, but are walk-ups. Many offer spectacular extended ridge walks. Most require you to leave the trail.

But there are a number with Forest Service trails to the top like Mount Wright, Steamboat, Lookout and Patrol Mountain, which are covered in detailed trail accounts elsewhere in this book.

The Front even shares the highest mountain in the Bob Marshall Wilderness Area, Rocky Mountain Peak (elevation 9,392 feet), that is a strenuous, but not a technical climb.

There is a general rule of thumb that most of these mountains have steep east faces but gently sloping west backsides. Many of these mountains are easily attained by selecting routes from these west slopes. Sawtooth (from Agropyron Flats) and Choteau (from Jones Creek) mountains are good examples.

What makes climbing in the Front so worthwhile are the views. Normally you can see out east onto the Great Plains, which resembles a great ocean punctuated by island mountain ranges like the Sweetgrass Hills, the Highwoods and laccoliths like Square and Crown buttes.

To the north, the great peaks of Gla-cier National Park are visible. Rising Wolf, Stimson and the great thumb, Mount St. Nick, come into view. To the west, all the way across the Bob, is the Swan Range with its tall, snow-covered peaks like Holland and Swan. But before the Swan you'll be on the lookout for the Chinese Wall, Pentagon, Silvertip and Great Northern peaks.

There is probably no better perch to view the Front and the Bob Marshall country than from Mount Wright.

The following is a sampling of how to climb some of the Front's more prominent peaks. But don't let this list stop you. The unnamed peaks and long ridgelines are innumerable. Let your imagination help you scale the heights.

Rogers Pass area

This is Continental Divide Trail country, where the path is well marked with giant cairns and signs on both sides of Highway 200. Rogers Peak (elevation 7,043 feet) is to the south along the trail about 1,400 feet in elevation gain and about 2 miles. Follow the trail to the north about 6 miles to Green Mountain (elevation 7,453 feet). Lewis and Clark Pass and the ridgeline above Falls Creek, including Red Mountain (elevation 7,277 feet), not to be confused with the nearby and higher Red Mountain (elevation 9,411 feet) in the Scapegoat Wilderness Area. These mountains can more easily be reached by taking the Alice Creek Road west of Rogers Pass to Trail No. 440 in the Helena National Forest. These provide an easy walk on grassy slopes and timbered trails.

Falls Creek area
Twin Buttes
Elevation: 7,532; 7,231 feet

East facing, climbable ridge accessible within 2 miles of Falls Creek Trailhead No. 229.

Caribou
Elevation: 8,755 feet

Long walk up the West Fork of Falls Creek (8 miles each way), straight up its steep, east face. The mountain can also be climbed from the west side of the Continental Divide up the Alice Creek Trail outside Lincoln or up from Indian Meadows.

Bear Den
Elevation 6,846 feet and
Monitor
Elevation 7,739 feet

Both are accessed from Falls Creek Trailhead No. 229. They are connected by a ridgeline that also extends to Twin Buttes. Hike 3 miles to where the West and East forks of Falls Creek meet and the trail divides. To the west and a bit north you'll see a saddle that leads to a ridgeline to gain Bear Den, whose top is marked with eerie monolithic rocks. Drop to a saddle and gain about 1,000 feet to the top of Monitor, walk the ridgeline back down to Falls Creek.

Table
Elevation: 7,163 feet

Accessed from Falls Creek Trail No. 229. Walk just beyond where the trail enters the national forest, study the flat-

On the way to Caribou, in the background, there was plenty of wildflower distraction.

topped mountain, with a burn on its flank, cross the creek and scramble 2,000 feet to the top up a broad ridge on the mountain's northwest flank.

Dearborn/Elk Creek
Steamboat
Eelevation: 8,286 feet

This is not the highest point on this long "Chinese Wall" type ridge, but it is the named peak. Walk up the main Dearborn River trail No. 206 about 1-3/4 miles to the Lewis and Clark Forest sign. Just beyond the sign and before a small drainage there is a pile of stones that marks a good game trail. There are ducks (small piles of rock) on this trail for a couple of miles before it peters out, but they will take you to a ridge that

Climbing Mount Frazier above the Blackleaf Canyon.

delivers you to a basin below the jumbled limestone outcroppings. The high point is the peak. It is higher than the large grassy peak to the east.

Steamboat Lookout
Elevation: 8,565 feet

Twelve-mile roundtrip climb from Elk Creek trailhead No. 205. It is all along an easy-to-follow trail. For more details see Steamboat Lookout Hike No. 4.

Haystack Butte
Elevation: 6,817 feet

This is a prominent landmark mentioned in the Lewis and Clark Journals and looms over the town of Augusta, sitting out in front of the mountains on private land. To access the mountain you'll need landowner permission. Best route: west ridge.

Benchmark/Willow-Beaver roads

Crown
Elevation: 8,401 feet

Ten-mile roundtrip climb from Benchmark Road. Take Crown Mountain Trail No. 270 to Petty Creek Trail No. 232 where you enter the Scapegoat Wilderness Area. In a short distance you are at the backside of the mountain and leave the trail, slogging up scree some 1,400 feet to the top. For more details, see Crown Mountain Hike No. 6.

Cyanide
Elevation: 7,900 feet

From the Wood Lake campground find Northwest ridge.

Fairview

Elevation: 8,246 feet

Climbable from Willow Creek Falls Trail No. 204. Once through the canyon, climb the peak from its west slope.

Patrol

Elevation: 8,015 feet

Ten-mile roundtrip climb on trail all the way from the Straight Creek trailhead at the Benchmark campground. The summit contains a manned Forest Service fire lookout. For more details, see Patrol Mountain Hike No. 7.

Renshaw

Elevation: 8,264 feet

Take Trail No. 256 up Benchmark Creek about 6 miles to where it reaches a ridgeline. Before the trail drops to Renshaw Lake, about a mile above its junction with Fairview Trail No. 243, leave the trail and gain the ridgeline that takes you to the top. Another way is to bushwhack up the drainage flowing into Renshaw Lake that eventually takes you to the top of the peak. For more details, see Benchmark-Renshaw Hike No. 8.

Gibson Dam/Sun Canyon Road

Arsenic

Elevation: 8,498 feet

At the Gibson Reservoir, Trailhead No. 201 connects quickly to Trail No. 252. Follow for nearly 4 miles to where Trail No. 259 comes in. Follow for another 1.5 miles, where Trail No. 251 comes in at a stream crossing. Begin immediately to look for an opportunity to gain a slope coming in from the west, which is the peak. Follow it up to the summit. Just below the top is a saddle

that often contains snow until August.

Grass Hill

Elevation: 8,172 feet

A nearly 7-mile walk up Hannan Gulch bottom at the Sun River to the north. The top of the ridge can be gained in many spots to the west, providing an interesting walk to the summit.

South peak

Elevation: 8,425 feet

From the Mortimer Gulch campground on Gibson Reservoir about 9 miles up Mortimer Gulch, follow Trail No. 251 to its junction with Big George Gulch Trail No. 252. Take the trail to the Bob Marshall Wilderness Boundary. It is a ridge walk from there.

Castle Reef

Elevation: 8,330 feet

Cross the Sun River on the bridge at Hannan Gulch. Turn right at the first road across the bridge. Pass several cabin sites, parking just beyond them. Proceed on a small trail into Wagner Basin. Once in the basin you'll see a ridge you can ascend to a saddle, which will take you to the top. The mountain can also be easily climbed from any ridge from Hannan Gulch.

Sawtooth Ridge

4 separate peaks: high point 8,179 feet

Easiest route is from Home Gulch, taking Trail No. 267 some 4 miles south to Agropyron Flats. Take the first open west ridge that leads to the base of the summit. It's a matter of working your way through several limestone ledges to the very narrow top. This is the top (elevation 8,135 feet) of one of four summits. The highest summit on this

The Steamboat ridge between the mountain and former lookout.

ridge is the third one to the south, before the yawning gap between the third and fourth peak. The scramble to the top is a sketchy hand-over-hand climb. For more details, see Home Gulch Hike No. 11).

Teton River Road (Main and South Fork)

Ear

Elevation: 8,580 feet

Starts from a BLM trail on the mountain's north side. When the trail runs out, look up and aim for a saddle between two points on that side. Once the saddle is attained, traverse to the mountain's south side. There is a well-worn game/hiker's trail through the scree and talus to a couloir that leads to the summit ridge. Watch for loose rock in this couloir. Just out of the couloir, there is a small but climbable point believed to be an Indian American vision quest site. There are several deep limestone sinkholes on top as well. Another way up this mountain is to start at the Ear Mountain BLM campground on the mountain's east side. Hike up a road for a short distance, looking up for a ridge that leads to the mountain's cliff-line. Go all the way to the cliffs, following their base to where it meets to game/hiker's trail at the bottom of the couloir on the mountain's south side. For more details, see Ear Mountain Hike No. 14.

Rocky Mountain

Elevation: 9,392 feet

The simplest approach is by way of Trail No. 165 to Headquarters Pass. Once in the great basin beneath the peak, there's a ridge running north from a saddle on the peak's east flank. Slog up that ridge through scree to the saddle and then negotiate the last several hundred feet of easy rock to the top. It is possible to climb the peak from Headquarters Pass up the north ridge as well, but it is more exposed. There are good goat trails on that ridge. You'll have to use your hands. Another route is to drop down the trail from the pass for about a half mile and look for the saddle coming off the peak's west flank. Climb through talus to that saddle and look for a route up the west side. It is also possible to scramble up the peak from Headquarters Pass. For more details, see Rocky Mountain Peak Hike No. 18.

Atop Mount Drewyer in the Swift Dam country with Mount Field in the background.

Cave
Elevation: 7,542 feet

About a mile up the Middle Fork of Teton Trail No. 108 from Cave Mountain campground, a drainage comes in from the north. Cross the stream and climb the mountain's south face to the top.

Choteau
Elevation: 8,398 feet

Begin at Jones Creek Trail No. 155. Study the mountain, and several west-facing slopes present themselves immediately. It is a slog up these scree slopes to the top, which is a narrow, walkable, glorious ridge. If you get on the ridge early, there will be several spots where you'll have to drop off the ridge to negotiate cliffs. Not far from the summit—on the north end of this long mountain – there's an exposed break in the ridge that you'll have to jump across

or carefully work your way across. Another scenic route is to take Clary Coulee Trail No. 177 for about 4 miles across the front where a climbable east ridge drops off the summit.

Old Baldy
Elevation: 9,156 feet

Take Route Creek Trail No. 108 up the Middle Fork of the Teton River 6 miles to the pass. At the pass gain the last 1,892 feet to the top up the mountain's north ridge. Another quicker and trickier off-trail route is to park at the Headquarters Pass-Our Lake trailhead. Just before the parking area there's a small creek that comes in from the north. Bushwhack through the forest just above that creek for about 1.5 miles to where the creek bottom opens up. This area is strewn with large boulders.

An aerial view of the Front west of Bynum.

You are at the base of the mountain now. Look up and find a ridge on the mountain's south face and follow the scree some 2,100 feet to the top. For more details, see Route Creek Hike No. 20.

Teton
Elevation: 8,416 feet

Up the South Fork of Waldron Creek, following a maintained snowmobile trail. In wet years there is a small lake in a broad, open area at the base of the mountain. Climb the ridge to the south and follow it to the summit ridge. There are several good game trails that lead to a saddle beneath that ridge.

Lockhart
Elevation: 8,691 feet

Start at the gated Waldron Creek cross country ski trail that is really a disappearing logging road that climbs into a basin at the foot of Lockhart's east face. A steep, broad ridge ascends to the south summit ridge right from the basin. Another more complicated way is to walk up the Waldron Creek road until it is crossed by a stream, about 1.5 miles from the gate. Abruptly leave the trail at this point and climb an increasingly steep and timbered ridge. When you can clearly see the summit, start looking for a game trail that leads to a saddle between Lockhart and the Teton Pass Ski Area mountain to the east. The saddle leads to Lockhart's east summit ridge, an interesting jumble of limestone cliffs. You can negotiate these by traversing to the north when they become too steep. Near the top there is a snowfield that doesn't melt off until August in most years. I'd recommend an ice axe on this snowfield. A number of Great Falls climbers like to traverse from Lockhart over to Teton on the ridgeline, something known locally as the "Lockhart Traverse."

Wright

Elevation: 8,875 feet

Eight-mile roundtrip hike with a 3,200+ foot elevation gain on a good Forest Service Trail No. 160 to the top. Offers some of the best views of the Front, Bob Marshall and Glacier Park. For more details, see Mount Wright Hike No. 23.

Wind

Elevation 6,917 feet

From South Fork of Teton County Road just beyond the forest boundary sign attain saddle, climb peak. About 1,500 foot gain from the road. If you go beyond Bear Creek, you've gone too far.

Blackleaf/North Fork Dupuyer Creek Roads

Werner

Elevation: 8,090 feet

Take Blackleaf Canyon Trail No. 106 to the pass above the East Fork of the Teton River trail. Leave the trail and proceed east. The mountain contains three peaks.

Frazier

Elevation: 8,315 feet

The most direct route is the mountain's south ridge, which can be reached by leaving the Blackleaf Canyon Trail No. 106 where it intersects. For those not comfortable with having to use their hands while climbing, a longer, but less exposed, route is to slog up the bottom toward a saddle coming off Frazier's west ridge. Attain the saddle; climb the ridge.

Old Man of the Hills

Elevation: 8,225 feet

Take Blackleaf Trail No. 106 to the cutoff trail to the South Fork of Dupuyer Creek No. 153. You'll cross a low, forested divide before dropping into the South Fork. Once at the South Fork, look for a southeast ridge that runs down from the mountain to the bottom. Climb to the ridgeline and gain the top. The mountain can also be climbed from the North Fork of Dupuyer Creek from Washout Creek.

Walling Reef

Elevation: 7,925 feet

Quickest way to climb this mountain is to access it from the North Fork of Dupuyer Creek road and canyon Trail No. 124. About 1.5 miles up the trail it intersects with Trail No. 150. Two miles up the trail, begin the hike up the scree to the east on the mountain's west face. Another longer and more difficult route is to start at Swift Reservoir, looking for the Phillips Creek Trail No. 150 that climbs to a divide between Walling Reef and the an unnamed reef to the north. Below the top gain the scree for the slog to the top.

Swift Dam area

Mount Richmond

Elevation 8,177 feet

This is the large mountain at the head of the Swift Reservoir. Best approach is from the North Fork of Birch Creek Trail No. 121. Look for Trail No. 105 cut-across trail, following it south across the creek. At the first opportunity, begin looking for the long ridge that leads up Richmond's northeast-facing ridge.

Coming off the Mount Lockhart spine.

Mount Sentinel
Elevation 7,680 feet

From Swift Reservoir take Trail No.105 to its intersection with the Middle Fork of Birch Creek Trail No. 123. There are several routes up where there are breaks in the limestone face

It is possible to get on the ridgeline itself and climb the peak.

Poia
Elevation: 8,274 feet and

Scarface
Elevation: 8,282 feet and

Morningstar
Elevation 8,376 feet

All three of these Blackfeet mythological peaks may be reached from the North Fork of Birch Creek Trail No. 105. Attain Poia by the ridge about a half mile west of Killem Horse Creek; Scarface, just beyond Small Creek. Morningstar can be climbed by continuing on the ridgeline from Scarface. It is possible to climb all three peaks on a long day.

Major Steele Backbone
Elevation: 6,749 and 7,004 feet

Best climbed by way of Haywood Creek trail/ATV road accessed from the north side of Swift Reservoir. The trail/road ascends about 1,500 feet to a saddle between the two peaks mentioned above. It is roughly 500 feet above the saddle to the north to the higher of the two peaks.

Badger-Two Medicine Wilderness Study Area

Heart Butte

Elevation: 6,863 feet and

Feather Woman

Elevation: 7,597 feet

South of the town of Heart Butte, look for Forest Service Road 9204, a rough, but passable gravel road that leads into the forest. When the going gets too tough, park; and on foot head for the pass between Heart Butte and Feather Woman Mountain. It is an easy scramble up Heart Butte's west-facing slope. The mountain is a sacred vision quest site for the Blackfeet. Be respectful as you see the brightly colored fabrics swaddling trees near the top. Descend to the saddle and climb Feather Woman up its east-face. Once you reach the ridgeline it is a short walk across outcropped rock to the top.

Kiyo Crag

Elevation: 7,655 feet

Find Forest Service Trail No. 172 at Palookaville outside the Blackfeet Reservation town of Heart Butte. It's on Forest Service Road 9128 which continues to the top of Mount Baldy! It is used to service the electronics equipment on the mountaintop. Some attain the Kiyo Crag ridgeline by driving to it. I recommend walking up Trail No. 172 for about a mile, studying the ridgeline and looking for a logical break to attain it, and then walking the 2,200 feet to the top.

Marias Pass

Flattop

Elevation: 6,549 feet

Elkcalf

Elevation: 7,607 feet

Both Flatttop and Elkcalf peaks can be reached from the Pike Creek Road on the west side of Marias Pass. It's a pretty good gravel road with large, but passable speed bumps on it. It winds its way for several miles coming to a spot where one of these bumps is not passable. This is where you get out and walk. ATVs use this route, so it is clear and easy to follow but not marked by any trail sign. It passes through a timber sale and the remnants of a burn from the 1980s.

The road crosses a stream and then heads up to a saddle where there is a trail well-marked by cairns. The burned over forest is with you all the way. To the south is Elkcalf; to the North is Flattop. Another way to climb Elkcalf is to find Trailhead No. 133 (which is more like an ATV road than a trail) in the Summit Campground. Follow it for 1 mile to its junction with Trail No. 137. The junction with the trail to the top comes in about 3 miles. For more details, see Marias Pass Hike No. 32.

Seldom-seen Alpine Lake from the top of Crown Mountain.

Special Areas Along the Front

National Recreation Trails

- Crown Mountain Trail No. 270
- Mortimer Gulch Trail No. 252
- Petty Crown Creek Trail No. 232
- Petty Fork Creek Trail No. 244
- South Fork Teton Blacktail Trail No. 168
- Jones Creek Trail No. 155
- West Fork Jones Creek Trail No. 156
- Part of the Front also contains the Continental Divide Trail

BLM Outstanding Natural Areas

There are four Outstanding Natural Areas (Blind Horse, Ear Mountain, Chute Mountain and Deep Creek/Battle Creek). These areas total 13,087 acres and are located on the Rocky Mountain Front about 20 miles west of Choteau.

Wildlife Management Areas

Blackleaf

Location: Northwestern Teton County, 15 miles west of Bynum; 85 miles northwest of Great Falls.

Even in late summer there's snow in the crevices of Mount Frazier.

Size: 11,107 acres.

Access: County road access from U.S. Highway 89 at Bynum. Main roads open year-round, as weather permits. Access to selected parking areas permitted from May 15 to Dec. 1, or July 1 to Dec. 1, depending on location.

Management Goal: To provide winter range for elk and mule deer, to prevent game depredation, to provide public access to WMA and adjacent public lands and to provide spring and summer habitat for black and grizzly bears.

Ear Mountain

Location: In western Teton County, 22 miles west of Choteau, 75 miles northwest of Great Falls.

Size: 3,047 acres.

Acquisition date: 1976.

Access: From State Highway 287 .5 miles south of Choteau, turn west on Bellview Road (at Pishkun Reservoir sign). Continue past the turnoff to Pishkun Reservoir (about 5 miles out) and proceed roughly 17 more miles to the trailhead on WMA's eastern border. There is no vehicular access inside the WMA.

Management Goal: To provide wildlife habitat for mule deer, bighorn sheep, grizzly bears and black bears and access to public lands along the Rocky Mountain Front.

Sun River

Location: In Lewis and Clark County, approximately 9 miles northwest of Augusta. The north edge of the WMA is south of the Sun River as it leaves Sun Canyon.

Size: 20,199 acres.

Freezout Lake.

Acquisition date: The first of 9 land purchases was made in 1948. The last purchase was made in 1974.

Access: From Augusta, take the Gibson Reservoir/Sun Canyon Road northwest approximately 3.5 miles. Where the road forks, take the left fork and proceed west 5 miles to the WMA. Vehicles may enter at the southeast corner of the WMA or 2.5 miles farther west at Swayze Lake. The WMA can also be accessed (walk-in only) at several turnoffs along the Gibson Reservoir Road.

Management Goal: To maintain and improve habitat diversity and quality for elk and other species currently utilizing the WMA and to provide hunting and wildlife viewing opportunities. In the winter, thousands of elk gather in the WMA and are often visible from the road.

Freezout Lake

Location: Teton County in north central Montana 40 miles west of Great Falls along U. S. Highway 89 between Fairfield and Choteau.

Size: 11,349 acres.

Access: Access to area from U. S. Highway 89 or Frontage road from Fairfield to various turnouts and parking areas year-round; interior roads open to vehicles March 15 to the beginning of waterfowl season annually; dike system roads closed to vehicles.

Management Goal: To provide habitat for waterfowl and upland game bird production and public hunting and viewing opportunity.

Sources: U.S. Bureau of Land Management, U.S. Forest Service, and Montana Department of Fish, Wildlife and Parks Web sites.

Hiking the Front with Children

The Rocky Mountain Front is an inviting place for families with young children.

It doesn't have the tourist distractions of a Glacier or Yellowstone national park.

For the most part, its roads aren't paved.

But that shouldn't stop you from enjoying one of Montana's most scenic areas.

Like the national parks, there are trails, waterfalls, picnic tables, camping sites, swimming and fishing holes, boating opportunities, horseback riding, dude ranches, fossil collecting, wildlife viewing, wildflowers galore, scenic drives and in the winter, downhill skiing, cross country skiing and snowshoeing, and snowmobiling.

Here are some suggestions for families

• Take a Montana Wilderness Association Wilderness Walk. There are usually more than 30 guided hikes offered in the Front. Contact the association's Island Range chapter in Great Falls or state office in Helena.

• Hunt for wildflowers in the spring on the southeast facing hillsides. The hillsides above the Dearborn River will be ideal in late June. (See the Devil's Glen hike No. 2).

• Visit a Forest Service Lookout. See hike No. 7 for Patrol Mountain.

• Take the scenic Benchmark-Willow-Beaver Creek-Sun Canyon Road Loop, and stop for a picnic at Home Gulch campground or have dinner at the Sun Canyon Lodge.

• Boat or canoe on Gibson Reservoir. The Sun Canyon Lodge offers rides to the end of the lake during the summer.

• Try horseback riding at one of the dude ranches along the Front.

• See a waterfall and have a picnic. Try Mill Falls or Cataract Falls (see chapter on waterfalls), both a short distance from where you park.

• Look for fossils in the hillsides. The mountains were once the bottom of a large inland sea. You can find sea shells in the white limestone rock.

• Go to Gibson Overlook; and while in the area, try a hike into Wagner Basin just below Castle Reef. A parking area with a rough trail into the basin is .7 miles from the Sun Canyon Road. Go to Hannan Gulch. The turnoff is .3 miles from the bridge to the right. Follow the road past a number of cabins another .4 miles. Just beyond the last cabin, park and it's about a 10-15 minute walk into this basin, where you'll see numerous beaver dams and possibly the bighorn sheep that live here. See hike No.12

- See one of the dams like Swift outside Dupuyer. There are camping spots and hiking trails nearby.

- Visit Roosevelt Memorial at Marias Pass west of East Glacier Park.

- Go to the Continental Divide Trail at Rogers or Marias Pass and hike along the trail, where one side drains toward the Pacific Ocean and the other toward the Atlantic Ocean.

- Visit one of the communities along the way. Augusta is a ranching town with a legendary rodeo in late June. Fairfield is near Freezout Lake Wildlife Management Area that attracts tens of thousands of snow geese and tundra swans on their Spring and Fall migrations. Try Choteau's active business district and Old Trail Museum. Bynum has a rock shop and dinosaur museum where you can arrange a fossil tour. Dupuyer is a cattle ranching town and near the Theodore Roosevelt Boone and Crockett Ranch. Heart Butte is an authentic Blackfeet Reservation community. East Glacier Park is as much a Rocky Mountain Front town as a Glacier National Park destination, with quaint and affordable tourist attractions and places to stay. It is also a good gateway to the Badger-Two

Medicine part of the Front.

- Visit the wildlife viewing areas. The Lewis and Clark National Forest ranger station in Choteau and supervisor's office in Great Falls have a pamphlet, "Wildlife Viewing on the Rocky Mountain Front." It suggests Freezout Lake, Pine Butte Swamp, Blackleaf Wildlife Management Area, the Theodore Roosevelt Memorial Ranch run by Boone and Crockett near Dupuyer and the Sun River Canyon for viewing a variety of wildlife.

- Wood Lake on the Benchmark Road is ideal for a picnic, fishing spot, hiking trail or campspot. It's on the Benchmark Road west of Augusta.

- Walk into the Bob Marshall or Scapegoat Wilderness Areas from one of the many trailheads off the Front.

- Go camping. There's never any competition for a spot at the Front's many campgrounds (See chapter on camping).

- Go fishing. Try the various reservoirs along the Front (See chapter on camping). Nilan Resevoir up the Benchmark Road outside Augusta has spectacular views of the Sawtooth Mountain country.

Skiing to the ridge line in South Fork Waldron near Teton Pass Ski Area.

⛷ Cross Country Skiing/Snowshoeing

The following hikes in this book make good cross country ski and snow-shoe trips:

- No. 1 Rogers Pass (suggest the south side of road to the top of Rodgers Mountain)

- No. 2 Dearborn River/Devil's Glen

- No. 21 Jones Creek

- No. 20 Middle Fork of Teton

- No. 19 Clary Coulee (start from the Teton Canyon Road rather than Blackleaf Canyon)

- No. 32 Marias Pass/East Flattop/Autumn Creek (Autumn Creek Trailhead is in Glacier National Park across the railroad tracks from the Visitor's Center on Highway 2. It runs east to Glacier Park Lodge, 15 miles away; and west, 7 miles below Little Dog and Elk peaks, dumping out on Highway 2).

Also, check out these areas of the Front for good skiing and shoeing:

Waldron Creek
North and South Fork drainages just south of Teton Pass Ski Area.

Lonesome Ridge:
Accessed from Middle Fork of Teton-Route Creek Trail (Trip No. 20). Can ski to top of ridge or down to South Fork of Teton River Road, sometimes difficult to reach when snow is deep or winds drift the road.

North Fork Teton out of West Fork
A main access point to the Bob Marshall Wilderness. Start where road is blocked just below Teton Pass Ski Area. Travel 3 miles and some 400 feet down to the bottom where the trail passes near the Forest Service Campground and West Fork work cabin and straight into the wilderness. Leave yourself enough energy to ski out and uphill.

West Fork
Same as North Fork Teton except look for West Fork trailhead before you cross the river to access the campground. Turn west where trail climbs toward Teton Pass skirting the southern flank of Mount Wright (a worthy goal itself).

Benchmark Road
Drive as far as you can go and ski up the road. Bighorn sheep are often on the road.

A rare winter rainbow while cross country skiing near Rogers Pass in the Front on the Continental Divide Trail.

Sun River Canyon:
Ski or shoe any of the parallel gulches that meet in the canyon, such as Home, Hannan and Norweigian gulches.

Camping

Forest Service Campsites

- **Benchmark,** 32 campsites, trailer spaces, drinking water, toilets, fee.

- **Home Gulch,** 15 campsites, trailer spaces, drinking water, toilets, boat launch, fishing access, fee.

- **Mortimer Gulch,** 28 campsites, trailer spaces, drinking water, toilets, boat launch, fee.

- **South Fork,** 7 campsites, trailer spaces, drinking water, toilet, fee.

- **Wood Lake,** 9 campsites, 6 picnic sites, trailer spaces, drinking water, toilet, boat launch, fee.

- **Cave Mountain,** 14 campsites, trailer spaces, drinking water, toilet, fishing access, fee.

- **Elko,** 3 campsites, picnic units, toilets, fishing access.

- **Mill Falls,** 4 campsites, trailer spaces, toilets.

- **Summit,** 21 campsites, trailer spaces, drinking water, toilets, fee.

- **West Fork Teton,** 6 campsites, trailer spaces, drinking water, toilet.

Other Public Campsites

- **Bean Lake,** 6 campsites, trailer spaces, toilets, boat launch, fishing access.

- **Nilan Reservoir,** 5 campsites, trailer spaces, toilets, boat launch, fishing access.

- **Pishkun Recreation Area,** 50 campsites, picnic units, trailer spaces, toilets, boat launch, fishing access.

- **Willow Creek Reservoir,** campsites, trailer spaces, toilets, boat launch, fishing access.

- **Eureka Recreation Area,** 10 campsites, trailer space, picnic units, toilets, boat launch, fishing access.

- **Bynum Reservoir,** primitive camping with 14-day stay.

- **Swift Reservoir,** primitive camping adjacent to the south of the Swift Dam spillway.

Other camping

- **Choteau,** 27 campsites, trailer spaces, picnic units, toilets, drinking water, fee.

Towns along the Front

Teton County Courthouse in Choteau.

Quaint western towns provide access points, supply stations and entertainment centers for the Rocky Mountain Front: Augusta, Browning, Bynum, Choteau, Dupuyer, East Glacier Park, Fairfield and Heart Butte.

Choteau (population 1,684), Fairfield (708) and Browning (1,016) are incorporated.

Browning, Bynum, Choteau, Fairfield and Dupuyer can be reached by U.S. 89, East Glacier Park by U.S. 2, Augusta by U.S. 287 and Heart Butte from the Birch and Badger creeks roads in Pondera County.

All the towns have a western cowboy feel to them, but the reservation towns of Heart Butte and Browning (the head of Blackfeet tribal government) are distinctively Native American. East Glacier Park is also on the reservation but is a Glacier National Park tourist destination.

Here are thumbnail sketches of what you'll find in these towns.

Augusta

This is a gateway town to the Sun River Canyon portion of the Front and Bob Marshall and Scapegoat Wilderness areas to the west. The skyline is dominated by Steamboat, Sawtooth and Castle Reef mountains and Haystack Butte. There are several small restaurants, bars, motels and an upscale curio shop where you can get a latté. The Lewis and Clark National Forest operates an information station. In late June the town holds a legendary rodeo. The 2010 U.S. Census indicates Augusta has 309 people. There are 666 people in the Augusta 59410 zip code. It is 52 miles west of Great Falls.

Browning

This town is a full-service community that serves as a jumping-off spot for Glacier National Park as well as the Badger-Two Medicine portion of the Front. The Blackfeet Reservation's Tribal Headquarters and Tribal College are located here as well as motels, restaurants, interesting curio shops and the Museum of the Plains Indian. In early July, there's a famous Indian powwow, North American Indian Days. The 2010 U.S. Census lists Browning's population at 1,016 people, but there are 7,719 people in Browning's 59417 zip code.

Bynum

This unincorporated town has a one-room schoolhouse, bar and colorful rock shop with a dinosaur museum, where you can arrange tours of nearby dinosaur dig sites. This is the access site for the Blackleaf Canyon. There are 96 people in the Bynum 59419 zip code.

Choteau

The biggest town on the Front and county seat of Teton County, Choteau offers full services and has a campground off the downtown, a tourist (Old North Trail) museum complex, motels, restaurant and a charming shopping area. Choteau provides access to the Teton River Road country, Teton Pass Ski Area, Nature Conservancy Pine Butte Swamp Area and ultimately the Bob Marshall Wilderness Area. Its Fourth of July activities include a rodeo and big-name country music entertainment. The 2010 U.S. Census has 1,684 people in Choteau. There are 2,643 people in the Choteau 59422 zip code. It is 52 miles northwest of Great Falls at the junction of U.S. 89 and U.S. 287.

Dupuyer

A pleasant stop with a community park, store, restaurant and gas station, Dupuyer is the entrance point for the Swift Reservoir area, the Theodore Roosevelt Boone and Crockett Ranch and the North Fork of Dupuyer Creek Canyon country. There are 104 people in Dupuyer's 59432 zip code, but the town is much smaller than that.

East Glacier Park is on the Blackfeet Reservation.

East Glacier Park

In the summer, this town is alive with Glacier National Park tourists who frequent its numerous motels, restaurants, gift and curio shops. A "must see" here is the Glacier Park Lodge, a magnificent resort built of enormous timbers which contains all the tourist amenities. During the winter, much of the community is shuttered, but basic services are still available like lodging and food. The community serves as a jumping-off point for access to the Marias Pass area, which is an entry-point to the Badger-Two Medicine portion of the Front. The 2010 U.S. Census indicates there are 363 people in East Glacier. There are 463 people in East Glacier's 59434 zip code.

The town of Dupuyer.

Heart Butte

This is a remote Blackfeet Reservation community that provides primitive access to the Badger Creek, Heart Butte and Kiyo Crag areas of the Badger-Two Medicine area of the Front on rough roads. Numerous fishing lakes abound here that require a Blackfeet fishing permit. It is wise to obtain a $10 Blackfeet recreation permit to use the area. The town's school complex is the community's centerpiece, but there is also a historic Jesuit missionary church located here. The 2010 U.S. Census indicates there are 582 people in Heart Butte. There are 743 people in Heart Butte's 59448 zip code.

Fairfield

Fairfield is an agricultural community that boasts it is the "Malting Barley Capital of Montana" because it supplies grain, irrigated by the Greenfield Irrigation District, to major brewers. The town is much more than this as a trade center with a golf course and swimming pool and full-service Main Street. North of Fairfield is Freezout Lake, that attracts hundreds of thousands of acres of migrating waterfowl, including snow geese and Arctic tundra swans. The backdrop for the lake is the Rocky Mountain Front. The most recent census lists Fairfield's population at 708 people.

Ridge above the Sun River Canyon.

Geology of the Front

What makes the Rocky Mountain Front such a breathtaking spectacle is also an interesting geology lesson.

It is here where the Rockies meet the High Plains that these mountains can be read like one might calculate the age and condition of a tree by counting and measuring its rings.

Geologist Bill Hedglin explains what happened geologically this way:

"Along the mountain front south of Glacier National Park, successive thrust sheets of Paleozoic (Cambrian through Mississippian) limestone grainstones and mudstones form the spectacular mountains and long ridges. These sheets were thrust up and over younger Paleozoic and Mesozoic rocks by compres-

sional forces originating far to the west where Pacific oceanic plates were colliding with and being subducted beneath (driven under) the continental plate to the east. This subduction is still proceeding today as illustrated by such features as the San Andreas Fault and the coastal range of volcanoes including Mounts Ranier, St. Helen, Hood, Baker and others.

"Within the front range south of Glacier Park can be found long, linear valleys situated between elevated thrust sheets of limestone. These features are called strike valleys due to their orientation parallel to adjacent mountain ranges. Examples of strike valleys include Hannan Gulch and Blacktail Gulch in the Sun River area. Green Gulch and Rierdon Gulch are prominent strike valleys farther north near the Teton River and associated drainages. Later glaciation also contributed to the current geometry of these valleys.

"Hundreds of thrust faults, with minor to major lateral displacement, have been mapped by many geologists since the early 1900s. The most well known of these faults is the Lewis Fault, visible in numerous areas on the east face of mountains on the eastern edge of Glacier National Park. This fault has placed Pre-Cambrian rocks, well over one billion years old, over the top of much younger Cretaceous and Jurassic rocks less than 200 million years old. This fault has been traced for considerable distance, both north and south of Glacier Park."

Hedglin, a native Nebraskan, has a bachelor's degree in geology from the University of Nebraska. He arrived in Montana in 1980, doing evaluation of structure and samples in oil and gas drilling operations along the overthrust. Later experience included overthrust work in several areas of Alberta. As an avid mountain climber, he's had 35 years of exposure to all types of rock outcrops in the Montana overthrust.

"Sometimes the arrival on the summit of a peak is delayed due to running across some fossil-laden strata on the ascent," he said.

"As the Pacific oceanic plates dove or were subducted beneath the continental plates far to the west, both hot igneous intrusive bodies (batholiths) and extrusive features such as volcanoes and lava flows were formed. All this tectonic activity resulted in compressional forces being applied on existing rocks to the east. As compression proceeded over time, deeply buried sedimentary rocks were buckled and pushed up over younger rocks, which is the definition of a thrust fault.

"Along the Front, continued eastward-directed pressure resulted in wave after wave of highly resistant carbonate sheets being stacked on each other in every angle from flat to near 90 degrees. An example of near vertical thrusting is Wind Mountain near the confluence of the South Fork Teton and the West Fork of the Teton River. Geologists have calculated this repetitive stacking of sediments resulted in some sheets being transported from 30 to 50 miles eastward."

This is his explanation of how various rocks in the Front were deposited:

"The carbonate rocks, limestone grainstones and mudstones within the Front were originally deposited in a shallow marine environment. During times of very shallow water, marine life was abundant, as proven by the presence of many fossils in some areas of outcrop along the front. These fossils include crinoids, brachiopods, several types of corals and other less plentiful species. In slightly deeper water, where fine grained carbonate mudstone was deposited, fossil frequency often decreases. Some of the older formations along and west of the Front also contain trilobites. Some of the younger Jurassic and Cretaceous sediments carried in the thrust sheets with older carbonate rocks can contain clam-like pelecypods, coiled ammonoid cephalopods (ammonites) and numerous other species of marine and non-marine life."

Mountain Names of the Front

From Lincoln to East Glacier Park, the mountains to the west tower over the Great Plains, separating Montana into east and west sides.

The Front serves as Mother Nature's canvas, receiving her palatte of colors delivered by the sun and clouds and their many moods.

After a snowfall, it can look like a giant strawberry sundae when flashed with sunrise pinks. During midsummer's dry spell, it is a stark golden wall. It is a purple mountain majesty after many a sunset.

But if San Franciscans know their Transamerica Building; New Yorkers, their Empire State Building; or Chicagoans their Willis Tower, many Great Fallsians would be hard pressed to identify these mountains by name.

From Broadwater Overlook on the hill with the Big Flag, the peaks of the Front unfold in a march to the north. On a clear day, Walling Reef west of Dupuyer is visible before the mountains turn the corner and go out of sight. However, some people swear they've seen Divide Peak from Great Falls as it juts off Glacier National Park outside St. Mary's. At best it might be Heart Butte, which has a similar shape. I know I've seen Chief Mountain on the Canadian border when I go to Choteau by way of a cut-off road from I-15.

The names in the Front are particularly interesting.

Shapes gave names

Some mountains are named for their shapes—outside Augusta there are Steamboat, Sawtooth, Ear, Castle Reef, Crown and Haystack. Beyond Bynum there's Old Man of the Hills, once known as Dupuyer Mountain.

Haystack Butte was called by its Indian name, Shishequaw Mountain, in Capt. Meriwether Lewis's journal in 1806.

The Front's highest peak is appropriately named Rocky Mountain Peak. The second-highest, adjacent on the horizon to the north, is Old Baldy, obvious for its high, above-the-timberline bald flanks.

Others are named for famous historical figures—(Willard) Werner, (Robert) Frazier, Patrick Gass, Drewyer (Drouillard)—all members of the Lewis and Clark expedition.

North ▶ Ear Mountain (8,580 feet) Rocky Mountain Peak (9,392 feet) Our Lake

From atop Mount Frazier looking north.

Then there are the not-so-famous: Mount Lockhart named for former national forest supervisor W.E. Lockhart, who died in 1931 while on official duties.

Mount Wright was named for a Capt. Wright who was in charge of tie or woodcutting operations on the head of the Teton River for the U.S. government around 1890. The wood was used to build Fort Assininboine near Havre.

One of the most prominent peaks on the Front, particularly in the winter when it is covered in snow, is Caribou Peak to the south of Steamboat.

Another peak, aptly named Fairview, is easily seen from Great Falls off the south flank of Sawtooth and provides those who climb to its top a truly fair view.

Memories are pretty dim about how some of these mountains got their names.

Old Baldy (9,156 feet)

Choteau Mountain (8,398 feet)

TAKEN FROM A FEW MILES NORTH OF C

While Mount Patrick Gass might seem obvious because of the connection to the Lewis and Clark Expedition, Forest Service records said it was named for a Lt. Patrick Gass, who worked under Wright cutting wood.

There are names the locals give them —Choteau Mountain is called Sleeping Giant because it looks like a reclining behemoth. Choteau (the proper spelling is Chouteau) was named in honor of Pierre Chouteau, Jr., president of the American Fur Co., who brought the first steamboat up the Missouri.

The Rocky Mountain Front marked the western limits of the Blackfeet Indians' territory, according to a 1993 Forest Service study.

Blackfeet Roots

The Blackfeet called the mountains along the Front "Backbone-of-the-World." In Backbone, lived Wind-maker, Cold-maker, Thunder, Snow-Shrinker (Chinook winds) and "spirits of the dead riding the wings of owls."
In the Badger-Two Medicine portion of the Front just west of Heart Butte and south of East Glacier Park, there are a number of the mountains with Blackfeet-inspired names.

There's Kiyo Crag; Kiyo is "bear" in Blackfeet. Bullshoe Mountain was named for a chief in 1883; Curly Bear Mountain for a noted Piegan warrior in the late 1800s; Little Plume Peak for a Piegan chief in the 1870s; Running Crane Mountain for a warrior of the Small Robes band in the 1840s-50s; and Spotted Eagle Mountain for the head medicine man in the late 1890s.

There's Morningstar Mountain. In Blackfeet mythology, Morningstar is the son of Sun and Moon and the identical twin of Scarface, a Piegan Indian god, for whom another mountain nearby is named. Then there are also Poia and Feather Woman mountains in the same North Fork Birch Creek drainage near Swift Dam, whose namesakes are part of the same Blackfeet legend as Morningstar and Scarface.

Terry Tatsey, who teaches natural resource management at Blackfeet Community College in Browning, noted that many of the mountains that we see from Great Falls were the hunting grounds for the Blackfeet.

Unfortunately, those names weren't written down, and some of the tribal elders were just small boys when they hunted with their parents and grandparents who would have called the mountains by the Indian names. Now some of the names are forgotten.

However, Rice Crawford of Heart

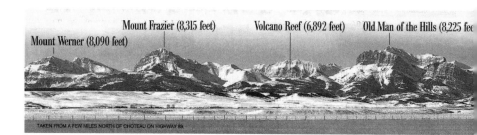

Mount Werner (8,090 feet) Mount Frazier (8,315 feet) Volcano Reef (6,892 feet) Old Man of the Hills (8,225 fee

TAKEN FROM A FEW MILES NORTH OF CHOTEAU ON HIGHWAY 89

Butte recalls that Walling Reef was called Bench Mountain by the Blackfeet when he was young. And Mount Richmond in the Birch Creek country was known as Paint Mountain because that is where the Indians collected materials to make paint.

Ear Mountain and Heart Butte were sacred vision quest sites where Indians went to fast and have a spiritual experience, Crawford said. Names like Sawtooth and Ear were common among the Blackfeet in his youth.

As with Ear and Sawtooth, which get their names from their shape, it doesn't take much imagination to understand where Teton Peak got its name.

That's the beauty of these Front peaks; they play to one's imagination. There are so many that are unnamed.

I'd like to see the prominent mountain to the north of Choteau peak named for A.B. Guthrie, the late Choteau writer and newspaperman who wrote the trilogy of frontier exploration books that included "The Big Sky."

Many of us already call the mountain that.

Some of us are already referring to the mountain separated by a ridge to the northwest of Ear Mountain as Metis Mountain in honor of the mixed breed Indians who settled the South Fork of the Teton River country below it.

Perhaps you'll find a name for one of these unnamed peaks when you venture there.

Walling Reef (7,925 feet)

◀ South

STUART S. WHITE/TRIBUNE

Related Resources and Maps

Here are the maps, book, and Web sites you'll want to navigate and enjoy the Rocky Mountain Front:

- Lewis and Clark National Forest website for maps and travel plans: fs.usda.gov/main/lcnf/home

- Bob Marshall, Great Bear, and Scapegoat Wilderness Complex, Flathead, Helena, Lewis and Clark, and Local National Forests, Montana Principal Meridian, 2012, USDA Forest Service Northern Region, $10 (Contains the index to Geological Survey Topographic Maps for the Front)

- BLM 1:100,000 scale topographic maps: Dearborn, Choteau, Valier, Cut Bank, Hungry Horse.

- Montana Atlas & Gazetteer, Topo Maps of the Entire State, DeLorme Mapping, Freeport, Maine, Pages 55, 69, 84 and 85.

- DeLorme, 3-D TopoQuads, Montana West.

- Montana Natural Resource Information System maps: nris.mt.gov Includes topos, land ownership and other useful maps.

- Montana's Bob Marshall Country, Rick Graetz, Montana Magazine, Helena, MT., revised in 2004

- Hiking Montana's Bob Marshall Wilderness, Erik Molvar, Globe Pequot Press, Guilford, CT.

- Crown of the Continent, the Last Great Wilderness of the Rocky Mountains, Ralph Waldt, Riverbend Publishing, Helena, MT.

- Montana and Idaho's Continental Divide Trail, the Official Guide, Lynna and Leland Howard, Westcliffe Publishers, Englewood, CO.

- Alliance for the Wild Rockies Web site: wildrockiesalliance.org

- Montana Wilderness Association Web site: wildmontana.org

- Coalition to Protect the Rocky Mountain Front Web site: savethefront.org/index.php

- Tom Kotynski's Web log: outtherewithtom.blogspot.com

U.S. Geological Survey
Topographical Maps of the Front

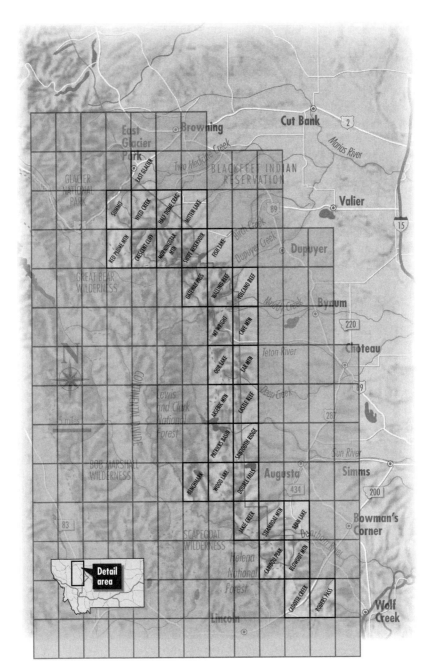

The Front Line

This book is a culmination of more than 40 years hiking in the Rocky Mountain Front and writing about these experiences in the *Great Falls Tribune* and on my blog, outtherewithtom.blogspot.com.

I've been joined on many of these hikes and mountain climbs by adventuresome souls who enhanced my experience and shared my joy.

There are some people who taught and pushed me, and without them this book would not have been possible.

Foremost among them is author H. Wayne Phillips, a retired Forest Service ecologist and botanist, who was a friend and neighbor in both Great Falls and Helena, and encouraged me to think beyond the narrow confines of trails. Without his instruction, the many mountains I climbed would have been out of reach and unthinkable; the many plants, flowers and trees along the way, unidentified.

Likewise, later on, Dr. Mark Hertenstein, a Great Falls chiropractor, became my climbing partner, and with him I share a love for the long traverse on forbidding ridgelines and peaks, and backcountry skiing, climbing and telemark adventures.

Bill Schneider of Helena, founder of Falcon Press, was an early inspiration. He and I shared many long backcountry hikes and runs, and I watched with awe as he churned out helpful, groundbreaking guidebooks that urge their users to respect and fight for wild country.

I continue to marvel at the dedication and energy of Bill Cunningham of Choteau. Author, teacher and conservationist, Cunningham has fought for wilderness protection throughout Montana and the Front for more than 50 years.

I don't think there is anyone more knowledgeable about or dedicated to the Front's preservation than Gene Sentz, a retired Choteau elementary school teacher. I've turned to him time and again for help, and his advice and direction have been invaluable.

Another major influence for this book was J. Gordon Edwards, the author of "A Climber's Guide to Glacier National Park," who died in 2004 at age 84 while climbing Divide Peak in the park. I embraced his book as my window on Glacier Park. It is filled with good descriptive writing about his adventures over more than 50 years climbing in the park.

Gloria Flora, the former Lewis and Clark National Forest supervisor, is an inspiration for her 1997 decision to protect the Front from new oil and gas leases for 15 years.

I deeply appreciate the support and encouragement of my wife, Katie, who early in our relationship encouraged me to write this, has edited this work, and has joined me on many of these trips.

Tom Kotynski, 2015

Tom Kotynski atop the limestone reef at the head of the West Fork Addition to the Bob Marshall Wilderness in the Front. (Mark Hertenstein photo)

About the Author

Tom Kotynski is a retired *Great Falls Tribune* editor and educator who has been hiking in the Rocky Mountain Front for more than 40 years. An active member of the Glacier Mountaineering Society, he has led climbs for that organization and hikes for the Montana Wilderness Association. He has climbed the six 10,000 foot peaks of Glacier, most of the Front's named peaks and many peaks within the Bob Marshall Wilderness complex. His blog is outtherewithtom.blogspot.com

Explore Montana

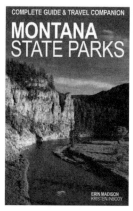

Montana State Parks:
Complete Guide &
Travel Companion

Montana Waterfalls:
A Guide for Sightseers,
Hikers & Waterfall
Enthusiasts

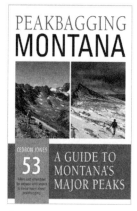

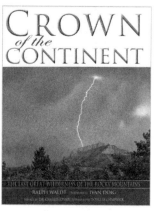

Peakbagging Montana:
A Guide to Montana's
Major Peaks

Crown of the Continent:
The Last Great Wilderness
of the Rocky Mountains

RIVERBEND
PUBLISHING

www.riverbendpublishing.com